W9-BGE-094

THE HOT NEW COOKBOOK FOR THOSE WHO CAN'T GET ENOUGH OF A GOOD THING

The ultimate turn-on for anyone hungry for love comes from New York City's The Erotic Baker®. THE EROTIC BAKER® COOKBOOK is a tempting collection of sexy recipes that are as much fun to prepare and look at as they are to eat.

Here are 100 fabulous recipes for: Baked goods that rise to the occasion . . . Appetizers for tasting and for play . . . Vegetables in the raw . . . Salacious salads . . . Orgiastic main dishes . . . And truly cheeky desserts. There's also a special section that will keep you abreast of the latest in erotic entertaining, as well as a miscellany of marvelous menus.

♥ Create a fabulous fantasy feast with the explicit, graphic instructions for Passion Pâté, Love Boats, Orgy Cakes, Finger Foods, Peel-Me-a-Grape Salad, and A-Hard-Man-Is-Good-to-Find Cream Puffs.

♥ Your New Position Office Party will never be a bust when you surprise them with a Blonde Bombshell Ambrosia.

♥ For a dish that won't be left behind, try whipping up a Fanny Fondue, or make your friends tongue-tied over scrumptious Trussed Chicken.

♥ Expose your guests to a Sunday Night Supper Orgy, or add your own magic touch to an Intimate Morning-After Brunch that will give special meaning to your parting "come again."

KAREN DWYER and PATRIKA BROWN are the owners and originators of The Erotic Baker®. Both live in New York City.

THE EROTIC BAKER® COOKBOOK

KAREN DWYER
&
PATRIKA BROWN

Illustrated by Joy Schleh

A PLUME BOOK
NEW AMERICAN LIBRARY

TIMES MIRROR
NEW YORK AND SCARBOROUGH, ONTARIO

NAL BOOKS ARE AVAILABLE AT QUANTITY DISCOUNTS WHEN USED TO
PROMOTE PRODUCTS OR SERVICES. FOR INFORMATION, PLEASE WRITE
TO PREMIUM MARKETING DIVISION, THE NEW AMERICAN LIBRARY, INC.,
1633 BROADWAY, NEW YORK, NEW YORK 10019.

Copyright © 1983 by The Erotic Baker®
The Erotic Baker® is the duly registered federal trademark of The
Erotic Baker®.
Illustrations copyright © 1983 by The New American Library, Inc.

All rights reserved

PLUME TRADEMARK REG. U.S. PAT. OFF. AND FOREIGN COUNTRIES
REGISTERED TRADEMARK—MARCA REGISTRADA
HECHO EN FORGE VILLAGE, MASS., U.S.A.

SIGNET, SIGNET CLASSIC, MENTOR, PLUME, MERIDIAN AND NAL
BOOKS are published *in the United States* by The New American
Library, Inc., 1633 Broadway, New York, New York 10019, *in
Canada* by The New American Library of Canada Limited, 81 Mack
Avenue, Scarborough, Ontario M1L 1M8

Library of Congress Cataloging in Publication Data

Dwyer, Karen.
　The Erotic Baker cookbook.

　1. Cookery.　I. Brown, Patrika.　II. Erotic Baker
(Firm) III. Title.
TX652.D9　1983　　　641.5　　　83-8356
ISBN 0-452-25439-6

First Printing, November, 1983

1 2 3 4 5 6 7 8 9

PRINTED IN THE UNITED STATES OF AMERICA

This book is dedicated to all our friends who have given their support and laughter freely, to all the Erotic Bakerettes and to all our crazy, wonderful customers.

We want to thank Suzanne Zavrian for all her help, advice, fun wit, and well-trained taste buds.

Contents

CONTENTS

Introduction

Food is one of life's erotic pleasures. Its wonderful colors and textures, its smells and tastes involve every one of our senses. Think for a minute of the different hues of a mango, from lemon yellow through deep red; the deep purple of a shiny, firm eggplant; the perfect shape and smoothness of a bursting-ripe red tomato; the soft, velvety blush of a perfect apricot.

Or think of the wonderful softness of bread dough as you begin to knead it; how the dough warms up as you work it; the warm, yeasty smell that begins to fill the entire house.

Then there's the texture and aroma of a perfectly cooked steak—the steam rising from it as you make that first cut; the brown and crusty outside, the pink center, and the wonderful juicy taste of the first bite as you slowly put it into your mouth.

A baked potato, soft and warm, as the butter melts in a golden puddle in the center of the fluffy mound . . . then you put a dollop of cold, white sour cream on top. If that isn't erotic, what is?

Or to focus more specifically—have you ever really *looked* at a mussel and seen what a tiny female sexual symbol it is? Or an oyster? Or a clam? No wonder they've had the reputation for centuries of giving sexual strength to the person who ate them.

Picture a hollowed-out squash, a cabbage cut in half; eggs, sunnyside up, quivering at you. Slowly peel a banana or look at a zucchini . . .

No doubt about it—food is sensual, sensuous, sexy—and as much fun to prepare as it is fun to eat!

We've always loved cooking, but in the beginning we weren't in the bakery business. Patrika was a Broadway lighting designer and Karen was an actress and singer. We both collected erotic art, and one day, as a joke, we decided to try making food that looked like some of the things in our collection. It worked! It worked so well that we began to entertain our friends by cooking erotic food from time to time, then more and more, until finally—*voilà!* in 1977 The Erotic Baker® appeared. And became internationally famous overnight. Radio, television, newspaper coverage, magazine articles; tours from the Far East dropping in; private planes from everywhere making trips to New York to pick up cakes—and by 1983, three stores doing a booming business.

And what a business! Respectable old Wall Street investment firms order cakes for office parties. A girlfriend of one of the players ordered an orgy cake for the New York Knicks basketball team, with the individual players on top —all in various positions and identified by their numbers. A meditation class ordered a rainbow-colored penis and pink breasts to celebrate the end of a 90-day celibacy period.

On the international level, there was the gentleman who wanted to bring back one of our cakes to his native Japan. In order to get it through customs, he packed it in a box with a false bottom. And then there was the customs officer in Milan who was so taken with one of our gingerbread men that he hung it up in his office.

We have "Humping Bunny" cakes for Easter; red, white, and blue vaginas for the Fourth of July, called "Birth of a Nation"; a "flashing" Santa for Christmas; and a cake with wedding bells known as the "Ding-Dong" cake!

INTRODUCTION

Of course, what's funny in the store is the way everything turns into a double entendre. The very first time a customer left and one of us trilled, "Come again . . ." we both turned fire red! But after a while, you accept it as just another occupation, like selling shirts and ties.

Well, not exactly like selling shirts and ties. There was the nattily dressed executive who spent a good half hour scrutinizing and comparing 30 to 40 hand-sculpted vaginas to pick out the perfect one for a friend. Or the woman who came back to tell us that the chocolate penis cake she had bought for her husband was just wonderful—except that he couldn't bring himself to cut it!

As you look at these recipes, you'll find it's very easy to shape various dishes to please yourself or someone else—or lots of someone elses! And great fun to combine shapes and colors and tastes. We have some suggestions in the back of the book to give you ideas for Erotic Entertaining on special occasions. We'll start you off with our ideas of what to combine with who or which, and once you get into the swing of it, you can make up your own Erotic Entertainments. You'll have as much fun as we had making things and putting them together, and even more fun serving them to your friends and lovers.

Karen Dwyer
Patrika Brown

APPETEASERS

This first section has recipes for food that will whet your guests' appetites, tease you into the main dish, and even be enjoyable all by themselves! These are all finger foods, small enough to eat in a bite or two, moist enough so that you simply have to lick your fingers afterward, and as enticing as foreplay.

But remember, save some room for the main dish— unless, of course, you're just teasing!

There's something wonderfully elemental about the taste of freshly ground beef—and alongside it, the sharp tang of capers, the bite of French mustard, the whiff of chopped onion, and the fresh green of newly chopped parsley. And whether you're having a buffet supper for 12—or an intimate dinner for 2, 6, or 8—this Appeteaser is the most expandable or contractible possible. (No pun intended!)

Beefy Parts
(Serves 3 to 4)

1 pound very lean round steak or sirloin, freshly ground
Salt to taste
Freshly ground pepper to taste

Capers
Chopped onion
Chopped parsley
Dijon mustard
Worcestershire sauce
4 raw egg yolks

Be sure and use freshly ground, very lean beef for this dish. If you wish, you can mix in the salt and pepper before shaping; however, we prefer to leave the beef *au naturel*, like the shapes. Everything else is served on the side, to be used as each guest chooses.

You can shape the beef in the following ways:

1. Make 4 round patties, carefully mounded up like breasts. Then make a shallow indentation in each one, just deep enough to hold 1 egg yolk. Very carefully place an unbroken yolk into each patty. These should be served in pairs, of course.

2. Shape a penis and testicles out of the beef, using the entire pound of meat. (see instructions, page 39). Serve the egg yolks on the side with the condiments, but place them in small, shallow bowls or dishes, and pair them for the right effect.

3. For an amusing and entertaining effect, shape 2 penises with testicles, using a half pound of beef for each. Indent each testicle, and place an unbroken yolk into each

indentation. When served to 4 guests, each gets one testicle and a half a penis—sorry about that!

When we serve this dish, especially if it's a buffet supper, we use an assortment of parts. It's very funny when they're all mixed together.

Serve the parts on a special platter (once we used a chopping board) decorated with sprigs of parsley, radishes, olives, pearl onions—whatever you choose to add. Arrange small dishes with the capers, chopped onion, chopped parsley, and mustard around the platter. Have a salt shaker, a pepper mill for freshly ground pepper, and a bottle of Worcestershire sauce. Guests mix the seasonings they want into their Beefy Parts.

Serve with toast, rye or cracked wheat bread, or any bread you prefer—and have fun!

Here's a naughty-but-nice Appeteaser.

Celery in Bondage
(Serves 6 to 8)

1 pound extra-sharp
  Cheddar, at room
  temperature
1 pound small-curd cottage
  cheese, at room
  temperature
1 tablespoon Worcestershire
  sauce

Pepper to taste
Pinch of thyme
3 small bay leaves (optional)
1 bunch celery
1 small spool twine or
  strands of rawhide

Blend the two cheeses together in food processor. Add the Worcestershire, pepper, thyme, and bay leaves and mix thoroughly. Place the celery on a cutting board and cut off the ends.

Wash and dry each individual celery stalk, and stuff with the cheese mixture. Press the stalks firmly back together, the smaller stalks inside, so that the bunch looks like it did originally.

Truss the ends of the bunch firmly with several strands of twine or rawhide. At 2-inch intervals wrap several strands of the twine or rawhide around the celery bunch and tie tightly.

Chill until firm, at least 2 to 3 hours. Remove the bound celery stalks from the refrigerator and place them on a cutting board and present them to your guests intact. Cut into ½-inch slices, removing the twine as you go, and serve the slices on buttered toast or on a rough rye cracker. They may also be served on a bed of lettuce with crackers or Swedish hardtack on each side. You may also top each slice with a teaspoon of Roquefort dressing.

NOTE: Wine-flavored Cheddar may also be used, or any sharp processed cheese of your choosing.

There's no way you can eat just one of these and stop! That's why we called them Cock-Teasers. The sharp, salty taste of the dried beef is the perfect foil for the creamy cheese, and the pearl onions lend the final fillip to your taste buds. It's best to make a lot of these—you'll need them.

Cock-Teasers
(Makes 8 to 10)

1 jar dried beef　　　　　**Pearl onions**
3-ounce package cream
　　cheese, at room　　　**Toothpicks**
　　temperature

Lay a slice of dried beef flat, spread it fairly thickly with cream cheese, and roll it up tightly. Secure the roll with a toothpick through the top, and spear a pearl onion on each end of the toothpick for testicles. Good things come in little packages!

Tasty, tempting, and tantalizing. That's our:

Devilish Whores d'Oeuvres
(Makes 12)

6 hard-cooked eggs
4 tablespoons mayonnaise
1 tablespoon mustard
Dash onion salt

1 small can mushroom
pieces, drained
Paprika
Capers

Split the eggs lengthwise. Remove the yolks and mash to a paste with the mayonnaise, mustard, and onion salt. Fill the egg whites with the mushroom pieces.

Fill a pastry bag with the yolk mixture. Using a #104 tube, with the wide end pointed down, start at the wide end of the egg and make two wavy ribbons, following the shape of the egg, around the mushroom filling. Sprinkle the yolk with paprika, and put a caper at the wide end of the egg.

NOTE: You can ignore the egg whites and just put an oval spoonful of mushrooms in the center of a small round of black bread and pipe the yolk mixture around it. Of course, don't forget the capers.

Served for Christmas, these could be St. Nick's Balls; at an Easter party, they'd be Bunny's Balls. But at any other time, they're just luscious old:

Furry Cheese Balls
(Makes 10 balls)

8 ounces cream cheese, at room temperature
Heavy or light cream
6½-ounce can minced clams
Worcestershire sauce to taste
Salt (optional)
Dash Tabasco (optional)
Chopped parsley

Soften the cream cheese with cream to a working consistency. Add the remaining ingredients, except for the parsley, and blend thoroughly. Shape into 1-inch diameter balls, and roll each one in chopped parsley.

This is a wonderful example of how many of the recipes in this book came into being. One day we looked at a whole pimiento as it came out of the can, and said, "It looks just like a French bra!" And before you knew it, the bra was filled with:

Mounds of Pleasure Cheese Spread
(Serves 10)

1 pound extra-sharp
  Cheddar, at room
  temperature
½ pound small-curd cottage
  cheese, at room
  temperature
1 tablespoon Worcestershire
  sauce
Dash Tabasco or
  horseradish

Pepper to taste
Pinch of thyme
1 can whole pimientos
Green olives stuffed with
  pimientos
1 radish
1 bunch parsley

Blend the two cheeses together in a food processor or blender. Add the Worcestershire, Tabasco or horseradish, pepper, and thyme, and mix thoroughly.

Line two small bowls with plastic wrap. (Bear in mind that the breasts will be the shape of whatever bowls you choose.) Pack the cheese mixture firmly into the bowls and either chill in the refrigerator for 3 hours or in the freezer for 1 hour until the cheese is very firm.

Unmold the cheese breasts side by side on the serving dish you plan to use. Remove the plastic wrap. There will be lots of wrinkles and cracks in the spread; put a little vegetable shortening or oil on your finger and, softly caressing, smooth out the imperfections.

Cut open a large pimiento so that it forms a bra cup. Support the bottom half of each cheese breast with a pimiento bra cup. Put an olive on top of each cheese mound to make a green and red nipple. Trim the radish into a

decorative shape and place it between the two breasts on top of the pimiento bra. Decorate around the radish with bits of parsley. You may also trim the top of the pimiento bra with parsley, too, if you like. The remaining parsley may be used to decorate the serving dish around the bottom of the breasts.

Use your imagination: almond pieces can be used to make white lace; the pimiento can be cut into strips to make bra straps and the strips may be alternated with parsley pieces for a lacy effect.

NOTE: This recipe can also be decorated the same way as Passion Pâté (see page 16). With all the red and green, this makes quite a decoration for a Christmas party.

Big, creamy mozzarella cheeses; the sharp, smoky taste of prosciutto—a simple, delicious Appeteaser that looks wonderful.

Mozzarella Mammaries
(Serves 8)

2 mozzarella cheeses
½ pound prosciutto or other thinly sliced ham

Pitted black or pimiento-stuffed green olives
Toothpicks

If the cheeses are oddly shaped, trim the edges with a paring knife to round them out—remember, there are very few perfect breasts! Carefully cut the cheeses into slices across, horizontally, then pile the slices back together again to re-form the rounded shape. Put a toothpick through the top of each cheese to hold the slices in place and spear an olive on the top of each toothpick for a nipple.

Arrange the ham slices in circles around each cheese in such a way that it will be easy to pull a slice out from under the cheese. The ham slices can overlap in the center, so that the cheeses can be placed side by side, almost touching.

If you like, decorate the platter with greens, radishes, olives—whatever takes your fancy. Serve with rye bread rounds and mustard.

This is perfect for molding into provocative shapes, and wait till you taste it! Not only will Passion Pâté satisfy your guests, it is also rich and filling. Serve it with rounds of rye bread, pumpernickel, or crackers, and you may never have to get to the main course!

Passion Pâté

(Serves 8)

2 hard-cooked eggs
⅛ pound butter
1 medium onion, chopped
1 pound chicken livers
1 teaspoon salt
¼ teaspoon pepper
2 tablespoons cognac
¼ teaspoon mace

Pimiento strips, cut ½ inch wide
Parsley
1 radish sliced in half
Pickle of choice
2 pearl onions
Olives stuffed with pimiento

Peel the eggs. Melt the butter and sauté the onion until soft. Cut the chicken livers into quarters and cook with the onions until done but still slightly pink inside. Put the

livers, onion, and eggs in a blender with the salt, pepper, cognac, and mace. Blend thoroughly. Taste and adjust the seasonings.

To mold

If you are going to mold a penis, chill the pâté first so that it is firm enough to work with, then shape by hand (see instructions, page 39). Chill as instructed below.

If you are going to shape breasts, you may also do it by hand. However, we find that the most successful way is to use two small bowls. (Keep in mind that the breasts will be the shape of whatever bowls you choose.) Line the bowls carefully with plastic wrap, pack the pâté in them firmly, and either chill in the refrigerator for 3 hours or in the freezer for 1 hour until the pâté is very firm.

Unmold the breasts next to each other on the serving dish. Remove the plastic wrap—you will see lots of wrinkles and cracks in the pâté. Put a little vegetable shortening or oil on your finger and, gently caressing the mounds, smooth out all the imperfections. Also smooth the breasts a bit into each other where the cleavage would be.

Now make a French half-bra with the pimiento and parsley. Use the pimiento slices to make the upper and lower borders of the bra. Cut off the stems of the parsley so that there is just about ⅛ inch left; put the parsley into the pâté between the pimiento strips, pushing the small stem ends into the pâté to hold the parsley. Top the pâté breasts with radish halves for nipples. Place a pickle between the two breasts with the pearl onions at the bottom end for testicles.

Decorate the plate with olives and the remaining parsley, making a circle of small bread rounds on top of the parsley, if desired.

NOTE: Pearl onions or olives may also be used as nipples; almond pieces can be used as white lace; experiment!

These may not look like fingers but they are the perfect finger food! Company's coming unexpectedly for drinks, and what can you do that's fast and fun? Well, if you've had the foresight to keep frozen pizza in the freezer, you can take it out, thaw it slightly, and make:

Piece-by-Piece Pizza

Frozen pizza
Pepperoni (or, in a pinch,
  salami)
Pitted olives

Take out the frozen pizza and thaw it slightly so that it can be cut with a scissors. Using the patterns for Spare Parts Sugar Cookies (page 125), cut out the pieces you want—penises and/or breasts.

Cover the pizza penis head and each testicle with slices of pepperoni. Put one circle of pepperoni in the center of each pizza breast, then center an olive half on each pepperoni circle on the breasts.

Heat according to instructions on the pizza package until baked through. Then eat your pizza, piece by sumptuous piece!

Here's a perfect example of using everyday things with imagination and fantasy. Take a round pita, cut it in half, open it slightly, and just look at it. You've got it! And it's perfect for stuffing with anything you like. (Well, almost anything!) We like to keep it simple and healthy—it's erotic-looking all by itself. So make an easy lunch out of:

Pussy Pita

Package of pita bread
Lettuce or a mixture of salad greens
Sliced tomato
Green pepper, cut in rings
Sliced Bermuda onion

Carrot curls
Quartered radishes
Sliced cucumber
Salad dressing (your favorite)

Slice each pita in half. Using any or all of the above ingredients—or any others you might fancy—fill each pita half and pour your favorite dressing over the salad ingredients. Have a pile of napkins on hand, and enjoy!

Sensuous but simple—here's an Appeteaser of small, shy breasts, blushing pink, with timidly quivering clear reddish nipples. It takes only cream cheese with pimiento, red caviar, and a little ingenuity.

Rosy Nipples

16-ounce container cream cheese with pimiento
1 small jar red caviar

Small rounds rye or black bread

Mound a small cream cheese breast on each bread round. Make a slight indentation at the top and put a dab of red caviar in it for a nipple.

NOTE: This can also be served in larger quantities for a buffet. Heap two large mounds of cheese on a platter, scoop out a good-sized indentation where the caviar is to go, and make large caviar nipples. Serve extra caviar in a dish on the side.

Instead of breasts, you can also make perfect little vaginas. Heap the cream cheese on the bread in an oval shape and hollow out the center, leaving two lips of cream cheese heaped on the outer edges. Fill the hollow with caviar. We suggest a silver platter for these.

Mamma mia! Bet you never saw pizza like this before! Frankly, neither did we, until one day when we had friends coming over for snacks, a pound of ground meat on our hands, and were feeling adventurous—so we came up with:

Stacked Pizzas & Pizza Picha
(Makes 4 breasts or 2 penises)

1 pound ground beef	1 ripe tomato, sliced thin
1 small onion, chopped	Tomato sauce
¼ teaspoon oregano	2 cherry tomatoes, halved
Pepper to taste	Mozzarella or provolone
Garlic salt to taste	cheese, sliced
2 English muffins	

Mix the ground beef with onion, oregano, pepper, and garlic salt. Taste and correct seasonings.

For Breasts: Slice the English muffins in half and toast lightly. Preheat the oven to 400° F. Top each muffin half with a slice of tomato. Heap a mound of beef mixture on the tomato slice in the shape of a breast. Spread a small amount of tomato sauce over the beef mound. Top with half a cherry tomato as a nipple and put into the oven for 15 to 20 minutes for medium-cooked meat. Remove from the oven and top with a slice of cheese; pop back into the oven for a couple of minutes until the cheese is melted.

For Penises: Slice the English muffins in half. Cut a penis out of one half of a muffin, rounding the end, of course. From the other half, cut two testicle shapes. Cut the tomato slices to fit the muffin shapes, then spread with the beef mixture as above. Heap the rounded end of the penis higher than the shaft, and round up the testicles. You can top each testicle with half a cherry tomato. Cover the meat with tomato sauce, as above, and cook for 15 to 20 minutes in a 400° F. oven. Remove from the oven and top with cheese cut to shape; put back into the oven for a few minutes until the cheese melts.

Teeny Weenies are small but potent. They're extremely easy to make, but they must be served with a straight face.

Teeny Weenies

Cocktail franks   **Mustard**
Pitted olives
Mayonnaise   **Toothpicks**

Steam the franks. Put a toothpick through one olive, then through a frank partway down, then through the second olive (see illustration). Mix the mayonnaise and mustard in the proportion of 2 parts mayonnaise to 1 part mustard. Top each frank with a little of this mixture, or use as a dip, if preferred.

Did you ever look carefully at a chick-pea? It's uncanny how much one resembles a tiny rear-end, and here's an entire canful of them with which to tease your guests.

Tiny Tushy Vinaigrette
(Serves 4)

½ to 1 teaspoon salt to taste
¼ teaspoon freshly ground
  pepper
2 tablespoons vinegar

1½ teaspoons Dijon
  mustard
6 tablespoons olive oil
16-ounce can chick-peas

Mix the salt, pepper, vinegar, and mustard. Using a fork, beat in the olive oil to blend well. Adjust the seasonings.

Drain the chick-peas and put them in a bowl. Pour the vinaigrette over, cover, and put in the refrigerator for several hours or overnight to marinate.

This recipe is for all you foot fetishists out there. It's dedicated to Peter, who turned us into toe-ticklers one hot Southern night!

Toe Tasters' Tasty Toes
(Makes 2 feet)

1 knockwurst
6 hot dogs
2 cocktail franks
8 ounces cream cheese, at
    room temperature
Milk or cream
Pink food coloring

1 package onion soup mix
Tabasco to taste (optional)
1 bunch radishes
Salad greens, preferably
    romaine
Crackers or bread rounds

Cook the knockwurst, hot dogs, and cocktail franks until done. Mix the cream cheese with a small amount of milk or cream to soften enough to work easily. Add a few drops of pink food coloring, the onion soup mix, and Tabasco, if desired. Mix thoroughly. Pile the cheese mixture into two mounds just high enough to hold the franks.

Cut the knockwurst in half and insert each half into the cheese to form big toes. Cut the hot dogs into descending lengths and insert next to the knockwurst for the middle three toes. Use the cocktail franks for little toes.

Clean and slice the radishes. The slices form nail shapes. For female feet, keep the red outside to imitate nail polish; the white inside should be used for male feet. Make tiny slits in the ends of the various sausages and insert the radish pieces into each slit as toenails. Garnish the plate with greens, piling them up around the cheese so that it looks as though the feet are growing out of the leaves.

Each toe can be removed by a guest and sucked, chewed, or just played with—whatever turns you on! And when you get tired of that, eat the cheese spread with crackers or bread rounds. Nothing goes to waste in this dish—it's quite a feat!

We love to make this recipe—it's basically a salad hors d'oeuvres bar, but not like any you've ever seen before! It's where you can let all your fantasies run wild. In fact, we usually only sculpt half the vegetables, then leave the rest piled on the side for our guests to experiment with. Talk about ice-breakers for a party—this is one of the best!

Vegetables in the Raw

All the following vegetables are uncooked:

Zucchini	Tomato
Radishes	Red and green peppers
Cauliflower	Bermuda onions
Carrots	Cabbage
Cucumber	Celery

Take a small, sharp paring knife and put your imagination to work. Zucchini and cucumber can be sculpted into penises; tomatoes and cabbage can be hollowed out. Green and red peppers and Bermuda onions make rings that carrots and cucumbers can be put through. Cauliflower florets are so erotic-looking in themselves that they serve as perfect side decorations—or whatever else you care to do with them. Just use your imagination—and let your guests use theirs. Try a real vegetable orgy. And once everything is sculpted and put together, dip the shapes into:

Honey-Pot Dip

1 head red cabbage	Radish
Russian dressing (1 cup mayonnaise to 1 cup chili sauce plus 1 tablespoon lemon juice)	Salad greens

Remove the center of the cabbage, making an oval hollow large enough to hold the dressing. Fill the center of the cabbage with the dressing, put a radish at the top of the hollow, and place the cabbage in the middle of the buffet. Arrange the salad greens around the cabbage.

P.S. We once held a Best-Sculpted Erotic Vegetable Contest, and Patrika's 83-year-old grandmother won the prize —a lifetime subscription to *Playgirl*. Her garden had produced a 4-foot zucchini just in time for the contest. She sculpted it appropriately, stood it upright in a giant hollowed-out squash, and walked away with the prize. That was one zucchini she didn't send to the church garden club!

THE MAIN AFFAIR

First, long, lazy drinks; then Appeteasers as intriguing lead-ins. It's all really foreplay to the main act— the main dishes. After all, that's what dinner's really about, isn't it? Appeteasers, erotic vegetables, saucy desserts—the Main Dish is a little like a Caliph surrounded by his harem of dishes—or a Queen of Sheba surrounded by her courtiers.

Think of all the messages you can get across with a Main Dish: Oyster Stew (I hope we get our strength back real fast!); Frogs Legs' Follies (this may be an intimate dinner for two, but I do have a sense of humor); a Cooked Goose, because it's all over, friend; or Kiss My Pork Butt because I'm still mad at you, damn it!

"The way to a man's (or woman's) heart is through the stomach . . ." Well, we're not so sure it is the stomach, so we just went ahead and invented a lot of dishes to have a go at it from all sides. Choose whatever suits the occasion—and if his or her heart isn't touched, at least their palates will be!

Everyone has one sooner or later! What is needed is something soothing—a long-simmering dish that already smells comforting even while it's cooking. Especially when it's a:

Broken Heart
(Serves 6)

2 veal hearts (about 1½ pounds each)
1½ cups stuffing (recipe below)
Flour
Salt and pepper
2 tablespoons shortening
1 carrot, diced
1 small onion, chopped
2 tablespoons chopped parsley
3 or 4 cloves
1 bay leaf, crumbled

1 small tomato, chopped
½ cup red wine
½ cup water

Stuffing
¼ cup butter
3 tablespoons chopped onion
3 tablespoons chopped celery
2 cups bread crumbs
Salt and pepper to taste
½ teaspoon thyme

Cut hearts in half in zigzag fashion (see page 31), but do not cut all the way through. Clean the heart by cutting away the fat, arteries, and connective tissue.

To make the stuffing, melt the butter; add the onion and celery and cook until soft. Add the bread crumbs and seasonings and mix well. Put half of the stuffing into each heart and sew shut.

Dust the hearts with flour, sprinkle with salt and pepper. Melt the shortening in a heavy saucepan; add the hearts and brown slightly, turning once or twice. Add the remaining ingredients. Cook, covered, very slowly for about 1½ hours. When done, put the hearts on a heated platter. To

serve, cut through the stitches so that heart falls open in a zigzag shape. Serve with pan juices.

A great platter for a party or a buffet supper, these are fun to make, fun to serve, and fun to eat. We experiment with different shapes before we fry them; then, sometimes, we experiment further with what can be done with the shapes on the platter after they're cooked. Try it—you'll think of things we never thought of! And probably things *you* never thought of either!

Cock-y Croquettes
(Serves 4 to 6)

1 pound canned ham or leftover cooked ham	1 medium onion, chopped fine
5 small potatoes, unpeeled	Bread crumbs
1 raw egg, lightly beaten	2 tablespoons butter

Put the ham through a meat grinder, or chop coarsely in a food processor. Boil the potatoes in their skins.

When the potatoes are done, mash them (leaving skins on) and add the egg, mixing thoroughly. Add the chopped ham and onion and mix well. Shape the croquettes in either male or female parts, or both. Carefully roll each "part" in bread crumbs; it may be necessary to pat them back into shape afterward.

Melt the butter in a frying pan until hot. Very carefully put the croquettes in the hot butter *in separate pieces.* That is, if you are making breasts, fry each one separately; if male parts, fry the penis shape and testicles separately. Turn once or twice carefully, and cook until brown.

When the croquettes are done, put them on a heated platter, putting the proper—or improper—parts together. In fact, you can put them so much together that your guests will hate to take them apart. And that's *very* Cock-y Croquettes!

You left her, she left you, you left him, he left you—either way, somebody's goose is cooked. Which calls for a dinner to celebrate your newfound freedom! What better way than with a:

Cooked Goose
(Serves 4 to 6)

8- to 10-pound goose
3 cups dried prunes
3 cups dried apricots

1 medium onion, sliced
Salt

Soak the prunes and apricots for about an hour in cold water. Drain the fruit and pit the prunes. Mix with the sliced onion. Preheat the oven to 350° F.

Rub the inside of the goose with salt and stuff with the fruit and onion mixture. Sew up the opening. Prick the legs and breast with a sharp knife. Put the goose in the pre-heated oven and cook, allowing 30 minutes per pound. Keep a kettle of water simmering on the stove during the cooking; baste the goose every 20 minutes or so with boiling water, removing the melted fat from the pan. When done, let the goose cool for about 15 minutes before carving.

 NOTE: The boiling water helps melt the fat. You will get at least a quart of fat; save it, as it's wonderful for cooking.

This recipe was invented by a very special friend, Donna. Ever since The Erotic Baker® began, she has been one of its most loyal supporters, and her standard line was always, "What are you doing over there, making penis pies?" So of course, what did we come up with but Donna's Penis Pie? It's a hearty dish for a cold night!

Donna's Penis Pie
(Serves 2 amply)

½ pound frankfurters
1⅓ teaspoons salt
½ teaspoon pepper
1 small onion, chopped
1 can tomato soup
   concentrate plus ⅓ can
   milk

1 medium potato, diced
1 medium carrot, diced
1 frozen, ready-made pie
   crust

Preheat the oven to 400° F. Slice the frankfurters in half, except for one, which is left whole. Put the sliced franks in

a casserole with the salt, pepper, vegetables, and soup with milk. Cover the casserole and bake for 30 minutes.

Remove from the oven and cover the casserole with pie crust. Cut a hole in the center of the crust large enough to insert the whole frankfurter. Put the frankfurter through the hole, leaving about half of it standing straight up outside the crust. Cover the exposed part with aluminum foil so that it doesn't burn. Perforate the crust in several places with a sharp knife so steam can escape. Put back in oven and bake another 40 minutes until the crust is brown.

Remove the foil before serving. Avoid arrest for indecent exposure.

Eve was tempted with an apple, but nobody's sure just how. So we thought we'd rewrite the story and give you our own version. You'll see what we mean, once you cook:

Eve's Temptation
(Serves 4)

4 medium-size cooking apples
Brown sugar

8 medium-size breakfast sausages

Preheat the oven to 350° F.

Pick nice, round apples. Core them all the way through. Slice each apple in half horizontally. Slice a small piece off the top and bottom so that they sit evenly. Place each slice, cut side up, in a baking dish. Sprinkle lightly with brown sugar. Put 2 or 3 tablespoons of water in the bottom of the dish.

Brown the sausages in a frying pan. When they are browned, insert one sausage straight up into each apple half. Put in the oven and bake for 40 minutes, basting occasionally.

If, when the apples are done, the sausages tilt because the apple pulp has become too soft, you can push the pulp around the sausages to hold them up. They should arrive at the table perky and erect, so that they really look like a Temptation!

These don't look exactly like the legs on the beauties at the Folies Bergère, but you'll be amazed at how real they *do* look. At any rate, they're not only good for a real laugh, they're real good eating!

Frogs Legs' Follies
(Serves 2)

8 small pair or 4 jumbo pair
   frogs legs
Milk
¼ cup flour
¼ teaspoon salt

¹⁄₁₆ teaspoon pepper
2 tablespoons butter
2 tablespoons oil
1 bunch parsley

Soak the frogs legs in milk for 1 hour. Mix the flour, salt, and pepper. Shake off the excess milk from the frogs legs and roll them in the seasoned flour. Melt the butter in a frying pan and brown the frogs legs, turning them often so that they don't stick. They take about 6 to 8 minutes to cook.

Place the frogs legs on a heated serving platter. Put a small bunch of parsley together and fan it out in the shape of a tutu. Using green thread, tie the bunch up near the leaves and cut off the stems. Put a tutu over each pair of frogs legs. Make sure the legs are arranged on the platter in a dancing line.

NOTE: If you're fond of the taste of garlic, it's much better—and more authentic—if, after you remove the frogs legs from the frying pan, you add a little finely minced garlic to the remaining butter and oil, cook it slightly, then pour the butter and garlic over the frogs legs.

So you've had your first fight . . . or your second. And, although you want to make up, you still feel that you should have the last word. Well, now you can. Invite him or her to dinner and cook our special:

Kiss My Pork Butt
(Serves 6 to 8)

3-pound pork butt   **3 tablespoons brown sugar**
Salt and pepper   **1 jar maraschino cherries**
½ cup water
Juice of 1 lemon   **Toothpicks**
1 tablespoon soy sauce

Heat the oven to 350° F. Rub the pork butt with salt and pepper. Put in a roasting pan with water and roast for 1 hour and 45 minutes, basting occasionally with a mixture of lemon juice, soy sauce, brown sugar, and pan drippings.

When the pork is done, let it sit for 10 to 15 minutes before serving. While it is waiting, remove stems from cherries and cut into quarters; fix with toothpicks in the shape of a pair of lips on the pork butt.

These are sensational: hearty and filling, with the elusive taste and smell of fresh, chopped dill, here are the lightest meatballs we've ever had. We think you'll become as addicted as we are to our:

Meaty Balls
(Serves 8 to 12)

1 pound ground beef	2 slices bread
½ teaspoon salt	½ cup milk
¼ teaspoon pepper	1 egg, lightly beaten
1 tablespoon fresh dill, minced fine, *or* ½ teaspoon crushed dill seed	Bread crumbs
	2 tablespoons butter
	Chopped parsley

Mix beef, salt, pepper, and dill. Tear bread into small pieces and soak in the milk. Once the milk is soaked up, add the bread and milk mixture to the meat with the egg, and mix thoroughly. (This works better if you mix with your hands, messy as it seems—and hand-mixing always feels good!) Shape into largish balls and roll in crumbs.

Melt the butter in a heavy frying pan. When hot, add the meatballs. Brown all over, then turn the flame down low, cover the pan, and cook slowly for 12 to 15 minutes, turning occasionally so the meat does not burn.

When cooked, sprinkle the Meaty Balls with parsley and serve in pairs on an oval bed of mashed potatoes.

NOTE: For the Russian version, add a few tablespoons of water to the frying pan and bring it to a boil, scraping up the meat fragments to make a gravy. When brown, remove from heat and add a spoonful of sour cream; stir in well. (Do not reheat or sour cream will curdle.) Pour sauce over Meaty Balls. From their size and heartiness, maybe we should have called them Cossack's Balls!

This is a wonderful recipe inspired by a former manager of our Village store, Doug. He was the genius who thought of adding that tiny touch that makes this recipe so special: cinnamon.

We've found this a great party-starter, made in different shapes and sizes and served buffet-style on a large platter. It's *very* interesting to see who picks which parts—and in which size!

Party Parts
(Serves 8 to 10)

2 pounds lean ground beef
½ cup Italian bread crumbs
½ teaspoon garlic powder
2 teaspoons Worcestershire
  sauce

½ teaspoon salt
1 small onion, chopped fine
1 egg
3 ounces tomato sauce
½ teaspoon cinnamon

Mix all the ingredients together thoroughly. Shape in a variety of ways:

Breasts: Heap meat up into two mounds. Make temptingly round. Nipples may be made of small white potatoes, green or black olives, cherry tomatoes, or radishes. Nipples should be added *after* meat loaf is baked.

Penises: Shape meat into a long cylinder with a shaped ball at one end for the head of the penis and two egg shapes at the other end for the testicles. *Or* you may use roasted potatoes for the testicles; we find that much funnier!

Place the Parts on a cookie sheet or an appropriate-sized baking pan(s) and bake at 350° F. for about 30 minutes.

Fastest gun in the East or West! Tough and sexy, and a lady to mess around with only at your own risk. Hot and spicy, she takes 'em and leaves 'em—this is:

Rachel's Cheatin' Heart Chili
(Serves 6 to 8)

2 pounds ground beef
1 teaspoon salt
2 teaspoons flour
¼ cup chopped onions
1 clove garlic, chopped
¼ cup olive oil

2 tablespoons chili powder, or to taste
¼ teaspoon oregano
2 cups canned tomatoes
4 cups water
2½ cups kidney beans

Sprinkle the beef with salt and flour. Sauté the onions and garlic in olive oil until golden brown. Add the meat, chili powder, oregano, tomatoes, and water. Cover and simmer until the meat is brown. Add the beans and cook over low heat for 1 hour.

Our friends always talk about our great gams. If you're a leg man or a leg woman, here's a real Gay Nineties dish for nostalgia fans. It'll practically do a high kick off the serving platter!

Stars and Garters Leg of Lamb
(Serves 4 to 6)

4-pound leg of lamb	Mint sauce
2 bay leaves, broken into pieces	6 medium potatoes
	Butter
3 fresh mint leaves or ½ teaspoon dried mint	Milk
	Salt to taste
Garlic powder to taste	Parsley
Pepper to taste	Pimiento or sweet red pepper
1 small onion, sliced thin	

With a sharp knife, cut incisions in various places on the leg of lamb. Insert pieces of bay leaf into the cuts along with the mint. Dust with garlic powder and pepper. Cover with onion slices.

Put the lamb into a 350° F. oven and roast for 2 hours. After the lamb has cooked for about 15 to 20 minutes, remove from the oven and spread with mint sauce. Return to the oven and continue cooking until done.

While the lamb is cooking, boil the potatoes. When they are cooked, mash them and add butter, milk, and salt. When the lamb is done, remove from the oven and place on a platter.

Shape the mashed potatoes around the upper part of the leg of lamb in the shape of a garter. If you have a pastry bag, use the #104 tube and pipe the mashed potatoes around the lamb. Be sure there are no lumps, or it will clog the tube. Put a frill of parsley above and below the potato garter. Add a star cut out of pimiento or sweet red pepper.

NOTE: This is great served with Cute Carrot Cocks.

As far as The Erotic Baker® is concerned, anybody can be seduced with a crisp, crackling brown duck. Any time. Any place. So go ahead and make our:

Suckling Duck
(Serves 4)

5- to 6-pound duck	**1 orange**
1 medium onion	**Salt and pepper**

Clean the duck thoroughly. Preheat the oven to 350° F. Cut the onion into wedges. Peel the orange and divide into sections. Rub the inside of the duck with salt and pepper, and stuff with onion wedges and orange sections. Sew up the cavity so that the pieces do not fall out during cooking. Prick the duck in several places to facilitate fat melting. Roast duck, allowing about 20 minutes per pound. If duck is very fat, remove excess melted fat during cooking. Duck may be turned once or twice during roasting.

Maybe it's your first date, and you've invited him—or her —over for dinner with friends. Or maybe it's their first date, and you've invited them to dinner with the two of you. Anyhow, *somebody* could use a not-too-subtle hint. And even if not, this is a fine beginning.

Sunny Chicken Breasts
(Serves 4)

4 medium boneless chicken breasts (or 2 large ones cut in half)
1 tablespoon butter
1 #8 can peach halves in heavy syrup

¼ cup orange marmalade
Maraschino cherries

Toothpicks

Preheat the oven to 350° F. Melt the butter in a frying pan and sauté the chicken breasts quickly until lightly browned. Arrange them in a baking dish, tucking them up

all around so that they look full and round, and bake, covered, for 25 minutes. While they are baking, drain the juice from the peaches and mix it with the marmalade.

After the 25 minutes is up, remove the breasts from the oven and glaze them with the marmalade and peach-juice mixture. Put a peach half in the middle of each breast, top with a cherry, and secure both with a toothpick. Return to the oven and bake for an additional 10 minutes.

These luscious lovelies can be kept hot in a chafing dish. And they go just fine with Virgin's Delight and Hot Hussy 'Taters.

Oysters have had a very special place in history, legend, and folklore: aphrodisiac, giver of strength, restorative, something practically magical for sexual power. Well, we do know for a fact that oysters have lots of iron . . . for the rest, if you believe it, it'll work!

Let's say it was a *very* long night, and *very* strenuous, and all everybody'd like to do is to go back to bed. But you have to get your strength back—or keep it up, whichever. So let us heartily recommend a tried-and-true remedy:

Superman and Wonderwoman Oyster Stew

(Serves 2 to 4, depending on amount of strength needed!)

1 pint oysters	½ cup cream
3 tablespoons butter	Dash Worcestershire sauce
1½ cups milk, heated	Dash paprika

Put the oysters, oyster liquor, and butter in a heavy pot. Heat gently until the edges of the oysters curl (5 to 10 minutes). Add the milk, cream, Worcestershire sauce, and paprika, and heat just to boiling. Serve immediately with an extra sprinkling of paprika.

Then go back to bed.

Serve the whole tongue on a platter. Tender, delicious, a teaser—just watch who you point it at!

Tongue Teaser
(Serves 6)

2- to 3-pound beef or calf's tongue	2 stalks celery, chopped
	6 to 8 peppercorns
1 medium onion, sliced	1 teaspoon salt
1 medium carrot, sliced	1 bay leaf

Scrub the tongue well, then soak in cold water for about 1 hour. Place in a kettle, cover with boiling water, add vegetables and seasonings, and simmer gently for about 3 hours until done. Let the tongue sit in the broth off the fire until cool enough to handle; then remove it from the kettle and skin it. Remove the gristle and any small bones from the root of the tongue. Return to the broth and reheat before serving.

Serve with Raisin or Horseradish Sauce.

Raisin Sauce

½ cup dark brown sugar	1 tablespoon lemon juice
1 teaspoon dry mustard	1½ cups water
1 tablespoon flour	Salt to taste
2 tablespoons vinegar	⅓ cup raisins

Mix the brown sugar, mustard, and flour. Add the vinegar, lemon juice, water, and salt. Cook over low heat, stirring constantly, for a few minutes, then add the raisins and stir until thick.

Horseradish Sauce

½ cup heavy cream	Salt to taste
3 tablespoons horseradish	

Whip the cream until stiff. Fold in the horseradish and salt. Chill until ready to serve.

It's S & M time! Celery in Bondage was a teaser, but for the main course, here's a young, plump, tender chicken, trussed so that she's helpless, at everybody's mercy, and just begging to be eaten! And there's a further surprise—inside, just to make sure that everyone's strength is kept up, is an equally plump, tasty oyster stuffing. You bite into the savory stuffing, and there's the special taste and special aphrodisiac attribute of oysters . . . some combination!

Trussed Chicken with Oyster Stuffing

(Serves 4 to 6)

4- to 6-pound roasting chicken

Stuffing
¼ cup butter
1 small onion, chopped fine
1 stalk celery, chopped fine

4 cups dry bread crumbs
Salt and pepper to taste
½ teaspoon poultry seasoning
2 cups oysters, cut into pieces
¼ cup oyster liquor

Rinse the chicken and dry it. Preheat the oven to 325° F.

To prepare the stuffing, melt the butter in a frying pan. Gently sauté the onion and celery until soft. Add the bread crumbs, seasonings, and oysters. Toss to mix. Add the oyster liquor and toss again. If not moist enough, add either more oyster liquor or a small amount of water.

Stuff the chicken and either sew up the neck and tail openings or close with metal skewers. Put the wings behind the back and tie together; crisscross cord over the body and tie the ends of the drumsticks together. The more firmly the lady is trussed, the better—don't overdo it and make the string too tight, however.

Rub the entire chicken with butter and roast, allowing 25 minutes per pound. Baste every 15 minutes with juices or melted butter. When done, serve on heated platter as is, and let whoever is the guest of honor cut the bonds.

People either hate them or love them, but we find something perversely sensual about kidneys—maybe it's their subtle, sharp taste, underlined by white wine—so rich it's the essence of erotic. Try them, you may become addicted!

Unmentionables on Toast
(Serves 4)

8 veal or lamb kidneys	**Salt and pepper to taste**
¼ cup butter	**½ cup white wine**
¼ teaspoon thyme	**8 slices toast**

Soak the kidneys in cold salted water for 1 hour. Remove the membrane, cut away duct and fat, and quarter each kidney. Melt the butter in a frying pan; when the butter is bubbling gently, add the kidneys, thyme, salt, and pepper. Cook for about 5 minutes, turning occasionally. Add the white wine and cook for 3 minutes more. Put the kidneys on hot toast, allowing 2 sections per person. Pour the juice from the pan over each portion of kidney. When it soaks into the toast, it almost makes a meal in itself!

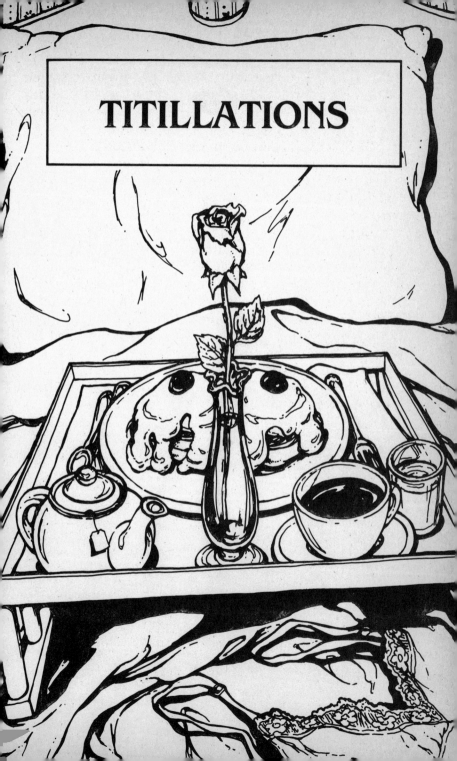

TITILLATIONS

This section is devoted to eggs, for obvious reasons. Watch two eggs frying, sunnyside up, gently bubbling away in butter. Look at them quivering shyly in the pan or on the plate when you serve them, as though they were afraid of being touched. Or take a peek at two poached eggs, bedded tenderly side by side in spinach or corned-beef hash and topped with capers or halves of small green olives. . . .

Whether you serve these egg dishes for breakfast, brunch, a light dinner, or a late supper, they'll be as titillating to serve as they are delectable to eat.

No, you're not a boob, silly! It's a "boob" omelet. Oh, you're not awake yet? Oh, never mind—just eat!

Boob Omelet

(Serves 2)

Filling
8 ounces cottage cheese, at
   room temperature
1 teaspoon fresh thyme *or*

¼ teaspoon dried thyme
Dash lemon-pepper
Salt to taste

Omelet
6 eggs
1 tablespoon water
1 teaspoon Worcestershire
   sauce

Pinch of fresh parsley
Salt to taste
2 tablespoons butter
1 green olive stuffed with
   pimiento

Mix the cottage cheese thoroughly with the thyme, lemon-pepper, and salt.

Beat the eggs lightly with water. Add the Worcestershire, parsley, and salt, and beat lightly again. Melt the butter and add the eggs to make the omelet.

When the omelet is done, slide onto a plate and make two nice, luscious round mounds of the cheese mixture next to each other on one half of the omelet. Slice the olive in half, place each half in the center of each mound. Serve on a hot plate, admire, and then fold the omelet and cut it.

Imagine two golden globes arriving at the table; you bite into one, it tastes of butter and herbs and has the consistency of a baked cloud. We guarantee this to be the most luscious, sensuous omelet to arrive at breakfast—or lunch —or any time!

Golden Globes Omelet

(Serves 2)

6 eggs, separated	**Salt and pepper to taste**
½ teaspoon tarragon	**4 tablespoons butter,**
½ teaspoon parsley	**divided**

Preheat the oven to 350° F. Heat two omelet pans or small frying pans. (Make sure they have heatproof handles.) Beat the egg yolks well with tarragon, parsley, salt, and pepper. Beat the egg whites until stiff and fold gently into the yolk mixture. Heat both pans; melt 1 tablespoon of butter in each, and pour half the egg mixture into each pan. Cook for a couple of minutes over a moderate flame, then put the frying pans into the oven. Bake for 8 to 10 minutes (less if you like runny omelets).

Melt the remaining butter. When the omelets are done, place them side by side on a heated platter and pour melted butter over them. Ummmm.

We love these Morning-After Breakfasts because they're hale and filling and have a little bit of everything—which we hope describes the night before. Besides, it's always fun to start the day with a giggle, and these'll get it for you.

Morning-After Breakfast I
(Serves 2)

4 sausage patties
4 eggs
1 tablespoon water
Salt and pepper to taste
Dash Tabasco or
    Worcestershire sauce

2 tablespoons butter
4 to 6 ounces cottage
    cheese, at room
    temperature
4 large capers

Fry the sausage patties on both sides until brown, keeping round shape. When the patties are nearly done, beat the eggs lightly with water, salt, pepper, and Tabasco or Worcestershire. Remove the patties from the pan and drain on paper towels. Melt butter in a frying pan, and scramble the eggs until they are desired consistency.

Put two patties on each plate. Mound a soft, swelling, cottage cheese breast on top of each patty. Top with 2 capers each for nipples. Heap up the buttery, fluffy scrambled eggs around the bottom half of each patty.

NOTE: Either as a variation *or* as an addition if you're hungry enough, fry up 4 sausage links. When they are almost done, in the same pan heat 2 cherry tomatoes for each sausage. Serve just like you think: 1 sausage penis, 2 cherry tomato balls—and heap up the scrambled eggs on top of the sausages and tomatoes like fluffy blond hair!

We must say we like to serve these all together, as it makes a remarkable-looking breakfast plate first thing A.M.!

Morning-After Breakfast II
(Serves 2)

4 slices ham, cut in rounds
2 English muffins, split in
  half

4 eggs
2 pitted black olives
1 cup Hollandaise Sauce

Fry the ham gently in a frying pan until heated through. Toast the English muffins. Poach the eggs in an egg poacher for 3 to 5 minutes (if you don't have a poacher, trim the whites to even them off). Cut the olives in half.

Put a slice of ham on each muffin half, top with poached egg, pour Hollandaise Sauce over each egg, and top with olive half.

Hollandaise Sauce

3 egg yolks
2 tablespoons boiling water
1½ teaspoons lemon juice

¼ pound butter, melted
¼ teaspoon salt
Pinch of cayenne pepper

Beat the egg yolks well in top of a double boiler over boiling water. Slowly beat in boiling water, then beat in the lemon juice. Beating constantly, add the melted butter very slowly, then the salt and cayenne. Continue beating until thickened.

NOTE: We still like to serve this occasionally with our sausage and cherry tomato cocks from the preceding recipe. Especially with each sausage inserted between a pair of muffin halves!

The following dish makes a fine brunch or lunch dish—or even a light supper. It's for one of those days when you're feeling lighthearted and silly because what this dish is going to provoke is revealed in its name:

Titters
(Serves 4)

1 pound spinach	**8 eggs**
2 to 3 tablespoons butter	**Pepper (optional)**
Salt to taste	**Cheese (optional)**
Pinch of nutmeg	

Wash the spinach carefully to remove any sand. Tear the leaves into smallish pieces and put in a pot to cook with just the water clinging to the leaves. Add the butter, salt, and nutmeg to the spinach. Cover and cook for 5 minutes, no longer.

While the spinach is cooking, cook the eggs very gently for 3 to 4 minutes in either an egg poacher or poaching ring. (If you do not have a poacher, you may trim the edges of the whites with a scissors to even them off.)

When the spinach is cooked, drain it thoroughly and make an oval-shaped spinach bed on each of four plates. With the back of a soup spoon, make two depressions side by side in the spinach beds large enough to hold one egg each. Put two eggs in each spinach bed. Sprinkle with pepper or cheese or whatever takes your fancy.

Variation: This dish can also be made with hard-cooked eggs. Shell each egg, slice it in half sideways, and put the white side down on the spinach bed so that yolk is looking up at you. (If it winks at you, don't blame us!)

This is a very special recipe for us—it's the brunch we were actually having the day the idea for The Erotic Baker® first came into being. But it's not here only for sentimental reasons—it's always been one of our favorite breakfasts.

One-Hung-Low Eggs

"The night before" get an order of either chicken or vegetable chop suey from your local Chinese restaurant. Or do as we do, and keep some frozen in your freezer. Make scrambled eggs, following the instructions in Morning-After Breakfast I (see page 53), for as many as needed. *(The ratio is 8 eggs to 1 portion chop suey.)* Mix the fresh, fluffy, buttery scrambled eggs with the hot chop suey for one of the best breakfasts you'll ever eat!

We serve this with fresh corn bread and our own Cheese Butter: In a blender, blend soft Cheddar cheese with softened butter—half and half. You can shape the butter as acorns or grapes in a butter mold if you'd like a special touch for what is really a very special breakfast.

LASCIVIOUS
LEGUMES

Vegetables can be among the most erotic things we eat. First of all, their shapes are so obvious that they divide neatly into two groups: on the one hand, cucumbers, zucchini, corn, asparagus; on the other, halved vegetables like avocado, acorn squash, red cabbage . . . Or are they what they seem? Look at our recipe for AC/DC Zucchini—you'll see what we mean!

Vegetables are also wonderful to look at—they're so colorful with their warm yellows and different shades of green, their reds and earth tones. It's a sensual experience just enjoying their colors! But there's also the smell—fresh tomato or just-picked corn, new spring asparagus and sharp, fresh shallots. Did you ever notice the feel of damp, silky mushrooms, or the crispness of very new string beans; the ultra-smooth deep-purple squeakiness of a perfect eggplant as you cut through the skin?

Or take corn on the cob. It's the perfect lusty vegetable: firm, large, sweet—and it's so obvious in its looks! You start with that first anticipatory bite—into the crisp freshness of the kernels, dripping with butter, then you begin to eat faster and faster, as if you can't get enough. It's a food you eat with your hands, so there's nothing between you and the corn: just the cob in your two hands, the smell of it in your nostrils, the crispness between your teeth as you bite down, and the buttery feel. That's erotic food!

This dish was invented one Christmas Eve, the first year The Erotic Baker® was in business. We had been up to our ears in cakes, cookies, and icing for 18 to 20 hours a day all the weeks before Christmas, and when Christmas Eve came, who had energy to go shopping and make a big, complicated dinner? So we took what was in the refrigerator, which just happened to be zucchini and chicken, and the result became The Erotic Baker®'s first Christmas Eve dinner!

It turns out to be a wonderful party dish. It works fine for a bridal shower, honeymoon meal, or just when you have a date and you're not quite sure . . . Here you serve this big, masculine-looking zucchini, lying proudly on the plate. Everyone is properly impressed. Then you open it up, and what have you got? A *very* female vegetable! We love to serve this to friends; it not only makes a satisfying meal, but it always brings on lots of laughs when we demurely announce that its name is:

AC/DC Zucchini
(Serves 2)

2 10- to 12-inch long
   zucchini
3 slices bacon
1 boned chicken breast, cut
   into chunks
2 tablespoons butter
¼ cup heavy cream
½ cup sour cream

2 teaspoons chopped red
   onion
1 tablespoon chopped fresh
   parsley
1 small radish
2 tablespoons grated
   Romano cheese
Paprika

Parboil the zucchini for 15 minutes. Let it cool. Fry the bacon slices, crumble, and reserve. Preheat oven to 350° F. Quickly sauté the chicken in the fat from the bacon. Transfer it to a baking dish and bake, covered, for 25 minutes.

When the zucchini is cool, melt the butter in a double

boiler. Add the cream, sour cream, onion, bacon pieces, and parsley. Add the chicken.

Split each zucchini in half lengthwise. Scoop out each half—leaving two of the halves much shallower than the others, which must be deeper in order to hold the filling. Fill the deeper two halves with the chicken mixture. Cut the radish in half and put a radish half at the top of each filled zucchini section. Sprinkle the two shallower zucchini halves with the cheese and paprika.

Put the zucchini halves in a 350° F. oven and bake for 10 minutes. When heated through, remove from the oven and place the filled halves gently on two plates. Top with the cheesed halves, being sure you remember which top half belongs to which bottom!

If you like, you may serve this surrounded by swirled mashed potatoes with lightly sautéed mushrooms, heads up, standing at attention. Well, standing erect anyhow!

NOTE: When very large zucchini are in season, you can buy the largest one you can find, and double or triple the filling recipe, cooking as directed above. (Parboil longer, however.) Once filled, it can be served with the zucchini doubling as a serving dish. Spoon out the chicken to serve, and slice the remaining zucchini in wedges or slices and serve on the side as a vegetable.

What's sexier than an artichoke, with its fabulous petals that take so long to eat? One petal coming off at a time, slowly stripping the artichoke down to its warm, soft heart. An artichoke was just made for seduction: each tender little petal is pulled off, dipped in butter or sauce, then slowly put into your mouth—or your partner's mouth—and the pulp gently scraped off. It's *really* sensuous, especially if you feed each other, but do it *very* slowly, and don't forget to lick the butter off your fingers at the end.

Artichoke Striptease

For this simplest of all stripteases, pick out young, firm artichokes. The petals should be closed tight. Remove the tough outer leaves and cut the bottom off the stem so that the artichoke sits level.

Boil 1 artichoke per person in boiling water with the juice of half a lemon until the outer leaves come off easily, about 30 to 40 minutes. When done, turn each one upside down and drain thoroughly. Stand the drained vegetable upright on a plate, and serve with a bowl of Lemon Butter (recipe follows) or Hollandaise Sauce (see page 54).

Lemon Butter

Melt ½ stick of butter, add salt and 1 teaspoon to 1 table-spoon of lemon juice to taste—and there's the easiest sauce this side of Paradise.

Here's a perfect luncheon dish, a light supper, or part of a bigger one. With a strong shaft of broccoli rolled up in pink cooked ham with ballsy red tomatoes and creamy sauce dripping off the end on the table, this is a *very* visual dish.

Big Bad Broccoli
(Serves 6)

6 stalks broccoli
6 small tomatoes
1 cup bread crumbs
2 tablespoons olive oil
1 teaspoon salt

¼ teaspoon pepper
12 slices cooked ham
1 cup Hollandaise Sauce
  (page 54)

Steam the broccoli for 10 to 15 minutes until barely tender. While it is steaming, slice the tomatoes in half horizontally. Turn each half over and squeeze gently to remove some of the seeds. Mix the bread crumbs, olive oil, salt, and pepper and spread a small amount over each tomato half. Put under a preheated broiler until brown, about 10 minutes.

When the broccoli and tomatoes are done, lay two slices of ham flat, the edges overlapping about an inch or so. Place the broccoli at one end of the ham, with the head protruding all the way out. Pour a thin ribbon of Hollandaise over the stalk, and roll it up in the ham slices. Put 1 or 2 more spoonfuls of Hollandaise over the broccoli head. Place 1 tomato half on either side of the ham and broccoli roll, so that they look like testicles. Repeat until all 6 stalks are prepared. Pop back in a 350° F. oven until heated through, approximately 15 minutes.

These big, white, creamy cauliflowers are perfect for a holiday treat. We often serve them for Thanksgiving or Christmas dinners—they're very good with Stars and Garters Leg of Lamb. They also make a good couple with Cute Carrot Cocks.

We've subtitled this a Bosom in Every Pot because neither of us has ever had a pot large enough to hold two cauliflowers—so we've had to put one bosom in each pot! Shy and delicious, peeping out of their sauce, these coy cauliflowers will never be wallflowers.

Coy Cauliflower
(or a Bosom in Every Pot)
(Serves 4 to 6)

2 perfect white heads of cauliflower	**2 tablespoons flour**
	¼ teaspoon salt
	Dash nutmeg
Sauce	**½ cup Parmesan cheese**
1 cup milk	**1 cherry tomato or 2**
2 tablespoons butter	**mushroom caps**

Remove the stems and leaves from the cauliflower. Steam them whole for about 20 to 30 minutes. Test from time to time, as you want the cauliflower tender and crisp, not soft.

While the cauliflower is steaming, prepare the sauce. Heat the milk in a saucepan. In another pot, melt the butter over low heat. Gradually stir the flour into the butter, using a wooden spoon, and cook for several minutes, stirring constantly. Add the hot milk very gradually, stirring all the while to avoid lumps. Cook for a few minutes more, still stirring, then season with salt and nutmeg. Stir in the cheese and simmer gently until the cheese is melted.

When the cauliflower is done, arrange the two cauliflowers on a heated platter and pour the sauce over and around

them, so that the soft, white mounds peep coyly out of the sauce. Top each bosom with either half a cherry tomato or a mushroom cap. We suggest you serve these shyly, with eyes lowered.

Here's the perfect Erotic Baker® recipe when you want to serve carrots: glistening, pearly white onions, bright orange, tapering carrots, the sweetness of honey, and just a whisper of ginger . . .

Cute Carrot Cocks
(Serves 4)

1 pound medium carrots	2 tablespoons honey
1 pound small white onions	Salt and pepper to taste
⅛ pound butter	Pinch of ginger

Scrape the carrots and peel the onions. Parboil both vegetables in boiling salted water until barely tender, 5 to 10 minutes. Melt the butter in a frying pan, add the honey, salt, pepper, and ginger. Cook for 1 or 2 minutes, stirring, and add the carrots and onions. Cook slowly for another 10 minutes, turning occasionally, until tender and well glazed.

Arrange each carrot on a heated platter with an onion on either side at the wide end. We guarantee a giggle with these—and they taste real good, too!

We like to serve these with Cock-y Croquettes, just to make sure our guests don't miss the point.

You want to serve something that's filling and comforting, yet intriguing enough to pep everyone up—something with a certain bite to it, an elusive, spicy flavor. So we came up with:

Hot Hussy 'Taters

Allow 1 good baking potato per person, and scrub them well so you can eat the skins, too, for an extra taste treat. Bake for about an hour in a 400° F. oven.

When done, slice off the tops of the potatoes lengthwise and very carefully scoop out the potato, leaving the skins intact. Mash the potatoes with milk and butter, adding salt and pepper to taste, until they are the consistency you desire. Then add hot horseradish to taste and mix well. Restuff the potato, mounding it up high, sprinkle with a little paprika for color and an extra bite, and put back into the oven until piping hot and slightly browned on top.

These will add pep to any meal!

We think of these in late fall, when the air smells of leaves and the first frost has arrived and you're hurrying home to a fireplace and someone you love.

Love Boats
(Serves 4)

2 well-shaped acorn, turban, or butternut squash
2 tablespoons butter, divided
2 teaspoons brown sugar, divided

1 teaspoon ginger, divided
Ground nutmeg
Pepper

Slice the squash in half (acorn or turban squash should be sliced around the middle; butternut sliced in half lengthwise). Take a thin strip off the bottom of each half so that it stands straight up. Scoop out the seeds and the stringy part of the flesh.

Put 1½ teaspoons of butter, ½ teaspoon of brown sugar, ¼ teaspoon of ginger, and a sprinkle of nutmeg and pepper in each squash half. Carefully put the halves in a baking dish; add ½ inch water to the dish, cover with a lid or seal with aluminum foil, and steam in a 350° F. oven for 45 to 60 minutes, depending on the size of the squash.

Serve warm and sweet and buttery and spicy—maybe with hearty Meaty Balls for a back-up.

Peter Piper Picked a Pot of Pecker Pudding—isn't that the way it goes? No matter—Pecker Pudding is a good pick to partake of with a perfect partner.

Pecker Pudding
(Serves 4 to 6)

6 sweet potatoes

2 tablespoons butter

½ teaspoon salt

½ cup milk

1 egg, lightly beaten

2 tablespoons sherry

Dash nutmeg

5 marshmallows

Boil the sweet potatoes until soft, about 30 minutes. Peel and mash them. Beat in the butter, salt, milk, egg, sherry, and nutmeg. Put in a casserole and level the top off as much as possible. Cut the marshmallows in half and make a row using 4 halves—this is the shaft of the penis. On each side at the top, overlap 2 halves to make the testicles. Split the remaining marshmallow and place in a V shape on the end for the head of the penis. Put the casserole in a 350° F. oven and bake until browned—about 25 minutes. After about 15 minutes, you may want to take the dish out of the oven and shape the softened marshmallows into a more realistic shape. If you do this, wet your fingers with cold water first, and be careful! Hot marshmallows are *very* hot!

When done, serve in the casserole.

These potatoes are probably blushing because they're mixed in with the carrots and, being modest, they're embarrassed. That's why we've called them:

Pommes de Terre Pudeur
(Serves 4 to 6)

1 bunch young carrots	Salt and pepper
6 medium potatoes	Paprika
4 tablespoons butter	Chopped parsley
⅓ cup milk, heated (or more, if needed)	

Peel the carrots and potatoes. Boil them separately, for about 20 to 30 minutes, until soft. Drain and mash. Mix well together, add the butter, milk, salt, and pepper and beat thoroughly. Mound onto a heated platter, sprinkle with paprika, and ring with chopped parsley.

Sometimes a dinner can be awkward at the beginning, especially if your guests don't know each other and everyone sits stiffly thinking up topics of conversation. The Erotic Baker® *much* prefers to start dinner off with something to liven up a party—with a giggle, not a blush! And one of our very favorites is this:

Potent-ate Potatoes
(Serves 6)

6 medium potatoes
3 tablespoons butter
½ teaspoon salt
⅓ cup milk or cream,
  heated

2 eggs
½ cup Parmesan cheese
Paprika

Peel and quarter the potatoes. Cook in boiling salted water until soft, about 15 minutes. Drain the potatoes and mash; beat in the butter, salt, and milk and whip until fluffy. Beat in the eggs and then the cheese. Taste and add more salt if necessary. Let stand about 30 minutes uncovered to dry out sufficiently to mold.

Preheat the oven to 350° F. Grease a cookie sheet with butter. Shape the potatoes into male parts (see Note below), brush with a little melted butter, and sprinkle more cheese and paprika over the molded potatoes. Bake for 15 to 20 minutes until lightly browned.

NOTE: We make this with a large male part, surrounded by a harem of little female parts. To shape the female parts, follow instructions for Devilish Whores d'Oeuvres (page 11).

Simple But Sensuous String Beans
(Serves 3 to 4)

Be sure and buy firm, crisp string beans. We cook these *al dente* because we don't want them to go limp on us. They need to be crisp, with their rich texture and color intact.

1 pound string beans	**2 tablespoons butter**
1 teaspoon salt	**Salt and pepper**

Heat a pot of water with the teaspoon of salt until it is boiling vigorously. Add the string beans and cook for about 10 minutes. Begin testing them at this point, and when they are the tenderness you want, pour them into a colander and rinse with cold water to stop the cooking process. When the beans are well drained, melt the butter in a frying pan or saucepan and reheat the beans in the butter with salt and pepper to taste until they are piping hot. (Be careful not to recook them.) They will be crisp, rich, and buttery.

Do you want to make dinner for a Super Stud—or a couple of them? Well, we have an idea for you, and it'll go just fine with Trussed Chicken.

Super Stud Potatoes
(1 per person)

Pick out a rough-looking yam and scrub it well. Rub butter into the skin and then sprinkle the yam with brown sugar. Wrap it carefully in aluminum foil and strategically stick 8 to 10 cloves through the foil into the potato. You can either put them in a ring around the end or the center, or just insert them wherever seems most appropriate. Bake at 400° F. for 50 to 60 minutes.

What's small, tender, and sweet, served up hot and steamy? Why, Virgin's Delight, of course!

Virgin's Delight
(Serves 3 to 4)

1 pint cherry tomatoes
4 tablespoons butter
1 teaspoon fresh or dried
  tarragon (preferably fresh)

2 tablespoons chopped
  parsley
2 teaspoons lemon juice

Melt the butter in a frying pan and add the tarragon and parsley. Cook for a minute, then add the tomatoes. Cook for about 5 minutes, shaking the pan frequently. Add the lemon juice at the last minute or so. (The tomatoes are done when the skins burst.) Serve in a heated dish so they stay hot.

SALACIOUS SALADS

Salads aren't just pieces of green stuff too big to fit into your mouth in polite company, they can be openers, side dishes, main courses, and conversation pieces. You can mold them, shape them, arrange them and, of course, eat them! Salads are fine for cold lunches, buffets, and especially for picnics.

The following are really fun to make, and they always attract attention and compliments—now that's not a bad combination, is it?

Musts for Molding

The following are suggestions for standard salad mix-tures that are perfect for molding. There are two rules to follow.

1. Be sure that everything is well drained before mixing, so that the mixture is dry enough to mold and keep its shape.

2. Chill the mixture completely while the mold is set-ting, and keep salads cold after they are set or mixed.

We are listing the ingredients for these recipes alone so that you can add to them or subtract, mixing the propor-tions to your taste. (Salads are perfect for experimenting.) Once mixed, you can mold these salads into breasts with small, rounded bowls or custard cups; pack the salad into them and chill thoroughly. Or you can shape any other parts you want by hand and chill well.

Chicken Salad

Mix together diced cooked chicken, minced onion, chopped celery, chopped parsley or dill, salt, paprika, and mayonnaise.

Egg Salad

Mix together chopped hard-cooked eggs, minced onion (approximately 1 medium onion to 12 eggs), fresh pepper and paprika, a dash of Worcestershire sauce, mustard, and mayonnaise. You can also add a touch of sweet relish. Be sure your eggs are very fresh.

Ham Salad

Mix minced canned or cooked ham with sweet relish, chopped hard-cooked egg, and mayonnaise. For a special taste, you can add some minced pineapple, but be sure it is very thoroughly drained and blotted on a paper towel, so that salad does not become too liquid.

Tuna Salad

Mix canned chunk tuna, minced onion, capers, lemon juice, and mayonnaise; for a very special touch, add finely minced fresh peaches or apples. Be sure the tuna is well drained.

The Amorous Avocado, with its subtle, musky taste and its smooth, damp texture, makes an ideal Appeteaser as well as salad dish. Let us warn you, however, that this recipe is definitely X-rated!

Amorous Avocado
(Serves 2)

1 large avocado
16 ounces cream cheese or farmer's cheese, at room temperature
2 tablespoons finely chopped dill plus dill sprigs for trim

Dash onion salt
Dash paprika
1 ounce red caviar
2 small black olives

Peel the avocado, cut it in half, and remove the seed. Mix the cheese, dill, onion salt, and paprika. Fill each avocado half with the cheese mixture. Using a #104 tube, fill a

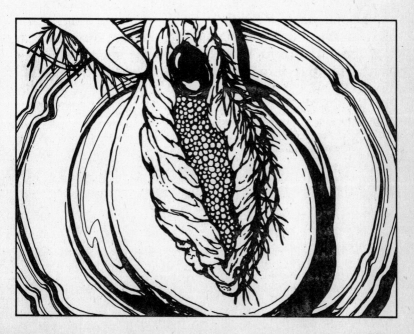

pastry bag with more of the cheese mixture. Pipe vaginal lips using the wide end of the tip, moving your hand up and down as you pipe the cheese out to make a ribbon of cheese along either side of the avocado edge (see illustration). Fill each center with ½ ounce red caviar. At the top of each hollow, put a small black olive. Trim all around the lips with fresh dill sprigs.

Definitely serve with Her Bread!

Aunt Patrika's Pickled Prickles
(Makes 4 pints)

12 4- to 5-inch cucumbers
3 medium white onions,
  thinly sliced
⅓ cup salt

2 cups wine vinegar
2 tablespoons sugar
¼ cup white mustard seeds
¼ teaspoon whole cloves

Slice cucumbers thinly lengthwise, place in an uncovered glass baking dish with sliced onions and salt and let stand at room temperature overnight. Drain the cucumbers and onions and wash in 2 cups of cold water and drain again. Mix vinegar, sugar, and spices together. Place sliced cucumbers and onions into 4 sterile, pint-sized mason jars. Pour vinegar mixture into jars equally. Seal and store in a cool place.

Serve this for a shower or put it in the middle of an hors d'oeuvres tray; it's also perfect for a surprise birthday party. For dessert variation, see Saturday Night Sundae (page 123).

Big Boy Banana with Big Girl Pineapple Salad
(Serves 1)

1 very ripe, firm banana
3 canned pineapple rings
Mayonnaise or whipped
  cream

1 maraschino cherry
Salad greens

    Stack the 3 pineapple rings on top of each other. Slice the end of the banana so that it will stand upright. Scoop out a tiny bit of the rounded end so that it will hold the cherry. Stand the banana upright in the center of the stacked rings, put a dollop of either mayonnaise or whipped cream in the top hollow, and stick the cherry on top. Put salad greens around the plate.

These lovelies may well blush—they're the sexiest tomatoes we've ever seen! They're great for a bridal or baby shower, a special lunch with something luscious, and they'll always make the perfect erotic picnic.

Blushing Boobs
(Serves 4)

4 medium, firm tomatoes
7-ounce can tuna, drained
2 tablespoons minced beets, either canned or cooked, plus 1½ teaspoons beet juice

2 tablespoons chopped red onion
Mayonnaise
2 cherry tomatoes, cut in half

Scoop out the medium tomatoes carefully, so as not to tear the skin. Mix the tuna, beets, and onion with enough mayonnaise to bind them together. Stuff the tomatoes with the mixture, heaping it up into high, rounded mounds. Top each mound with half a cherry tomato.

This is a perfect salad to serve in spring or early summer —preferably for a Mae West type, demanding, "Peel me a grape!"

Peel-Me-a-Grape Salad
(Serves 2)

1 medium fresh pear, peeled
3 ounces cream cheese, at
   room temperature
1 drop pink food coloring
1 teaspoon crystallized
   ginger, finely chopped

1 tablespoon milk
Ground nutmeg
Powdered cinnamon
1 pound seedless green
   grapes
Salad greens

Slice the pears in half, remove the seeds, and blot pear halves dry. Soften the cream cheese with food coloring and milk, then mix in the ginger. Spread the mixture over each pear half. Sprinkle with nutmeg and cinnamon. Cut the grapes in half and stick them flat side onto the cream cheese close together so that the finished decoration looks like a bunch of grapes. Place leafy greens at the top to resemble grape leaves.

This is really lovely when finished, and so decorative you'll hate to eat it!

Sexy Surprising Salads

With a bunch of open-minded friends who are ready for fun, this is a great party game! It would be wonderful for a Halloween party—especially since we got the idea from a friend who once came to a Halloween party dressed as a salad; he was the hit of the evening!

If you have a willing (or long-suffering!) friend, that's the best and funniest way to do this. If not, either make a painted cardboard cutout of a figure or see if you can rent a department-store mannequin.

We're giving directions for this recipe using a live person. It will be even simpler for anything else you use.

Salade de Bonne Femme

Chicory

Parsley

Carrot curls

Iceberg lettuce

Cherry tomatoes

Tomato slices

Raw cauliflower

Broccoli

Salad dressing of your choice

Bread slices

Pats of butter

Have your female model lie down on a table and cover her hair with a bathing cap or plastic wrap.

Starting at the top, create hair from the chicory and parsley. Arrange it into a hairdo, using carrot curls for blond highlights. The same combination can be used for pubic hair, skipping the carrot curls, if you prefer.

Tuck the iceberg lettuce all around the body, creating a bed of lettuce. Then place half a cherry tomato over each nipple (making sure the tomato isn't too chilly, or it might pop off!); cover the breasts with slices of tomato. At the neck, wrists, and ankles make tropical jewelry by alternating cauliflower and broccoli rosettes, similar to a Hawaiian lei. Pour a little salad dressing into the navel, then tuck a gravy boat between the knees and fill with the remaining dressing. Arrange slices of bread down the arms and legs, and place butter pats on the stomach, radiating out from the navel.

As your guests make their way around the table, they can pick and choose as they please, and dip their salad pieces into the dressing. However, No Tickling Allowed, and please—ask the salad *not* to sneeze!

Salade de Bon Homme

For the male version of this salad, the instructions are the same except for one small (or possibly large) thing: because of certain problems that could pop up, you may want to tie a plastic bikini over the pubic area. If so, substitute a cucumber, two tomatoes, and some parsley to give a similar and edible effect. On the other hand, you may not want to tie the salad down with a bikini—that's up to you (no pun intended).

The method of eating either of these salads is entirely up to you and your guests—but DO NOT TOSS!

This is to serve just before something begins—like a long-awaited affair, or any time you're feeling amorous. Because it's:

Suspended Animation Salad
(Serves 4)

The following quantities are for four people—you can increase them for larger numbers, of course, and put several fruit arrangements throughout. You may vary the Jell-O flavor, but be sure and choose one that is light and clear.

2 packages lemon Jell-O   **1 pear half**
3-inch firm banana slice   **1 fresh, canned, or**
2 small apricot halves   **maraschino cherry**

Prepare the Jell-O and refrigerate it until it is just firm enough to support the weight of the fruit. Place the banana slice into the Jell-O with one apricot half on each side to serve as testicles. Put the pear half into the Jell-O with the cherry at the wide end. Arrange the fruit so that the banana is heading toward the pear, in a state of Suspended Animation.

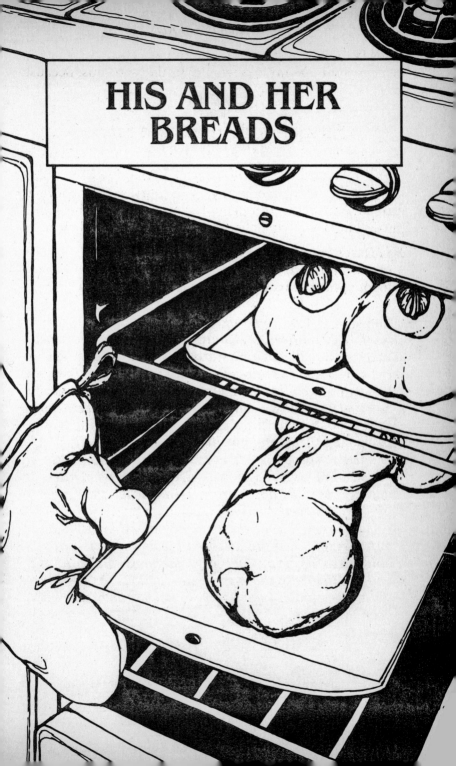

HIS AND HER BREADS

They call it the staff of life. Well, we do too, except maybe our idea of "staff," isn't exactly what they had in mind. We not only have bread for him at The Erotic Baker®, but bread for her, too. Our bread is one of the first things we carried and it's still one of the best sellers in the store.

That really pleases us, because making bread is one of the most sensuous, erotic things we know. The wonderful yeasty smell of rising bread that fills every room; the softness of the dough as you plunge your hands into it; its smooth, elastic feeling as you work on it; the silkiness as it starts to tighten up. Even the sheen on the dough as it starts—what else?—rising.

Both he and she will love His and Her Bread. Everyone will—even the older generation. One day a sweet-faced little old lady came into The Erotic Baker®. She spent about 10 minutes picking up His Bread loaves, inspecting them, and putting them down. Finally one of the salespeople went over to her and said gently, "Excuse me, but maybe you don't know what these loaves are?" "I know perfectly well what they are," the lady snapped. "But are they salt-free?"

If you really don't have time to make bread, look around and see if pre-prepared bread dough is available. Then you can skip the actual dough preparation and go directly to the shaping instructions. As Patrika says: "If you don't have time to knead the bread but need the bread . . ."

Dough
(Makes 1 loaf)

⅓ cup sugar
2 cakes compressed yeast
2 cups lukewarm water
1 tablespoon salt
6½ cups sifted all-purpose
   flour, divided

2 eggs
⅓ cup shortening

For Her Bread Only:
2 walnuts (in shell) or
   kumquats or gooseberries

Mix the sugar, yeast, and water in a mixing bowl. Add the salt and 2 cups of flour. Beat with an electric mixer for 2 minutes. Add the eggs and melted shortening and beat for 1 minute. Gradually add the remaining flour, stirring until a dough is formed. Allow the dough to rest in the bowl for 20 minutes. Place dough on a floured board and knead for 10 minutes.

How to Shape

His

1. Place the dough on a floured board. Divide it as follows:
2. Form A into a long loaf.
3. Pinch in the end to form the head.
4. From C and D, form the balls. Attach them to A by pushing the dough slightly into the A shape.
5. Form a skinny string from the B dough. Place this on top of the shaped dough to make a vein.
6. Gently lift the finished shape onto a greased baking pan. Let rise in a warm place for *1 hour.*
7. Brush with beaten egg and bake at 375° F. for 30 minutes.

Extra-Tasty Ideas
1. Make him into a hero sandwich to share.
2. While he's still hot, brush him with whipped honey for breakfast or a late-night snack.

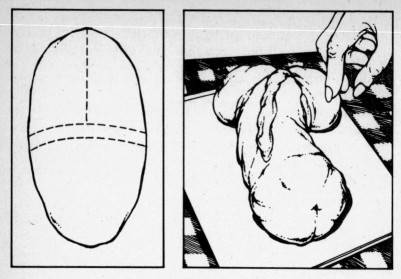

`    `3. Split him gently down the center, insert butter and garlic, and heat him up.

Her

`    `1. Place the dough on a floured board. Divide the loaf as follows:

`    `2. From A, form two attached mounds.

`    `3. Divide B in half and push gently into the center of the mounds to form nipples.

`    `4. In the center of each nipple, insert a walnut (in shell), kumquat, or gooseberry.

`    `5. Gently lift her onto a greased pan and let rise in a warm place for *1 hour.*

`    `6. Brush with beaten egg and bake at 375° F. for 30 minutes.

Extra-Tasty Idea

A glaze of warm marmalade over this beautiful warm bread will make an unforgettable breakfast. Hot chocolate or café au lait in bed with your breasts—perfect!

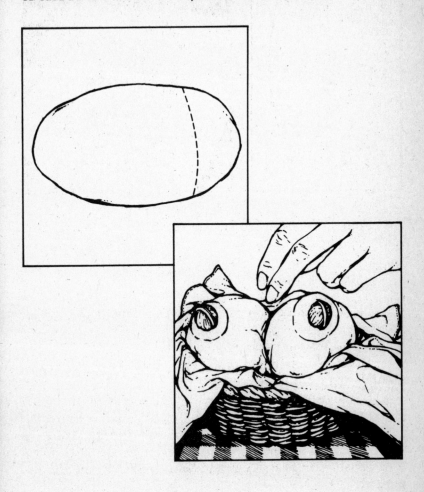

THE CLIMAX

We're coming to the end of the meal, but it's just the beginning of the evening! And it's the best part of the meal to really let your imagination run wild with your craziest fantasies: whipped-cream bras and peachy asses and cherry nipples and cookie words and licorice whips . . . it's all ahead of you.

The blessing of dessert is that nine times out of ten, you can prepare it way ahead so that you really have the chance to lavish not just imagination but time and care on the dish. Read through the entire section, and don't be afraid to play around. If you want a Happenis Cake with ice cream balls, be our guests! Or maybe you'd like a Chastity Chest-nut Puree turned into a Macho chest-Nut Puree. Dip up your Fanny Fondue with funny Four-Letter Cookie Words—we could go on and on, and you can, too.

Try taking your very favorite desserts and thinking up ways to make them into your own erotic recipes. It's all in your fantasies, so if you can fit your favorite recipes and your favorite fantasies together, wow! And if, on top of it all, you have a sweet tooth—like we do—there'll be no stopping you. You might even end up a Master Baker!

Assorted Balls and Nuts

We have balls and nuts for all occasions. Snow Balls, Witch's Balls, Leprechaun's Balls, Health Nuts, Real Nutz, and Numb Nuts. It's fantastic to make up a platter of all these recipes for a big party—they're all so simple to do. Take small sticks—like ice cream pop-sticks—and glue stickers to each one with the name of the recipe on the stick. Success guaranteed! Especially after your guests taste them. So on with the balls!

~ Balls ~

Snow Balls
(Makes 12)

9-inch baked yellow-cake
  layer
¼ cup corn syrup
1 tablespoon lemon juice
½ teaspoon grated lemon
  rind

4 tablespoons marmalade or
  raspberry jam
2 cups flaked coconut

Crumble the cake and mix with corn syrup, lemon juice, lemon rind, and jam. Form balls about 1½ inches in diameter. Roll in coconut until completely covered.

Variations:
Santa's Balls: If you make Snow Balls for Christmas, just change the name to Santa's Balls and serve them with Rudolph's Balls.
Leprechaun Balls: Use green coloring for St. Patrick's Day to turn Snow Balls into Leprechaun Balls. Put the coconut into a plastic bag, add several drops of green coloring (careful—one drop at a time), and shake vigorously until all of the coconut is colored. Make the balls much smaller—leprechaun size—and roll them in the green coconut.

Witch's Balls: For Halloween, use orange food coloring and follow directions in Leprechaun Balls for coloring the coconut. You may also cover six of the Witch's Balls with the orange coconut and roll the other six in chocolate jimmies.

Patriotic Balls: For the Fourth of July, cover four of your balls in red coconut, four in blue coconut, and of course, cover the last four in white. You might try putting a small flag on top of the pile of balls, which should be mixed.

Rudolph's Balls
(Makes 12 balls)

2-pound fruitcake
⅓ cup corn syrup
2 tablespoons rum

2 cups flaked coconut
Red food coloring

Crumble the cake and mix with corn syrup and rum. Form balls 1½ inch in diameter. Put the coconut into a plastic bag with a few drops of the red coloring and shake vigorously until all of the coconut is colored. Roll each ball in the coconut until completely covered.

This is a recipe that brings customers back to The Erotic Baker® again and again—it's so addictive, it must be illegal! It must be started at least one week in advance to allow the raisins to soak long enough in rum.

Rum Balls
(Makes 12 balls)

½ to ¾ cup rum
1 teaspoon rum flavoring
½ cup raisins (approx.)
9½-inch baked chocolate
   layer cake

¼ cup chocolate frosting or
   corn syrup
2 cups chocolate jimmies

Mix the rum and the rum flavoring in a measuring cup. Put the raisins into a bowl and pour rum over, covering raisins completely. Let soak for 1 week until the raisins plump up with rum. (*Note:* Patrika says 1 week; Karen says 2 days!)

Crumble the cake and add the raisins and ¼ cup of the rum mixture. Mix with frosting or corn syrup. Be careful mixture does not become too sticky; it should form easily into 1½-inch-round balls. Roll in jimmies to cover.

~ *Nuts* ~

Health Nuts
(Makes 15 1½-inch balls)

2 cups peanut butter
½ cup molasses
1½ cups yellow raisins
½ cup dried milk powder

2 cups chopped unsalted
peanuts, walnuts, or
pecans

Combine the first four ingredients. Form them into balls and roll them in the chopped nuts. Chill.

Several years back, a well-known sex manual advised applying crushed ice to strategic places at strategic moments. That gave us a terrific idea for a super dessert.

Numb Nuts
(Makes enough for 2)

1½-ounce bag sliced
almonds
½ cup coconut

1 pint coffee ice cream
Amaretto

Crush the almonds and mix with the coconut. Using an ice cream scoop, make two balls of coffee ice cream. Set the ice cream balls side by side in a shallow bowl or dish with the almond–coconut mixture nestled around them. Pour a small splash of Amaretto over the Numb Nuts.

This recipe is sensational! It's delicious, simple to make, and you can whip up large quantities at one time. They're the perfect present (wrapped in a plain brown bag, of course) to say nothing of using them for parties, favors, or just to keep around the house. But we warn you, they won't last long.

Real Nutz

1 pound shelled walnuts	**½ cup granulated sugar**
2 egg whites	**4 tablespoons cinnamon**

Beat the egg whites to a froth. Mix the nuts with the whites until the nuts are thoroughly coated. Put the sugar and cinnamon into a bag and, mixing half the nuts at a time, shake the nuts in the bag with the sugar mixture until covered. Turn the nuts onto a baking sheet and bake in a 350° F. oven for 20 minutes, or until the cinnamon and sugar adhere to the nuts.

Here's a wonderful dessert for a warm night. Outside it's hot and steamy and the air's faintly scented; inside, dessert is the fresh taste of fragrant melon, the sharp cold of sherbet, and the crunchiness of toasted coconut. Except that dessert *looks* as hot as the night, because it's:

Blonde Bombshell Ambrosia

1 ripe canteloupe
1 pint sherbet: cranberry, boysenberry, or strawberry (must be pink or red)

½ cup toasted coconut
2 purple grapes

Slice the canteloupe in half. Scoop out the center of each half in an oval boat shape. Fill the hollow with sherbet. Outline the edges of the hollow with toasted coconut to simulate pubic hair. Place a grape at the top of each hollow.

Some prefer tops, some prefer bottoms. For the latter, here's a dessert that's pretty, perfectly rounded, firm, and a guaranteed turn-on!

Brandied Bottoms
(Serves 3)

1-pound can cling peach halves
½ cup brandy, divided

½ teaspoon cinnamon
½ teaspoon nutmeg
Cloves

Put the peaches with about half their syrup into a saucepan with ¼ cup of the brandy and the cinnamon and nutmeg. Heat gently until the peaches are heated through. On a heated serving platter, pair each two halves of a peach together to form perfect bottoms. Insert a clove between each pair; you'll have to stick the end of the clove into the edge of a peach half to hold, but it will still look as though it were directly in-between.

Heat the other ¼ cup brandy and pour it over the peaches, lighting it immediately. Serve flaming hot!

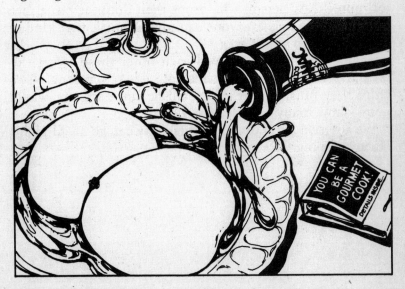

Here's the dessert of desserts, X-rated and *strictly* for the adventurous:

Brett's Fanny Fondue

Chocolate Sauce	*Things to Dip*
3 tablespoons heavy cream	Pound cake squares
1 ounce Grand Marnier	Banana pieces
12 ounces bittersweet chocolate, grated	Kiwi fruit pieces
	Strawberries
1 ounce Cointreau or kirschwasser	Orange sections
	Mandarin orange sections

Use a fondue pot, and heat the sauce mixture according to fondue pot directions. Make sure the room is well heated, too, because your guests will be baring their bottoms. We use a low table for this dessert (dessert game is more like it) with lots of cushions around it. Bare bottoms are on the cushions, and each guest takes a turn dipping a piece of cake or fruit into the fondue pot. (Banana pieces are our favorite—they're erotic *and* delicious; who could ask for more?) Any person who drops their dunking piece into the pot has to kiss everyone's fanny. Or if it's that kind of party, they can spank, too.

Sometimes our guests feed each other these sweet tidbits; if someone dribbles chocolate down someone else's chin, they must lick it off. You'd be surprised—or would you?—how many accidents there are.

We advise a *lot* of fondue—this party can go on all night! Happy dipping. . . .

Warm brown breasts, fluffy white bra, stand-up nipples, and the sweet, delicious, nutty taste of chestnuts with vanilla whipped cream: just who could resist this luscious dish? (And if you like quickies, and this seems like too much trouble, find a good gourmet shop and buy either sweetened pureed chestnuts or unsweetened puree and add sugar syrup and vanilla to it.)

Chastity Chest-nut Puree
(Serves 4)

1 pound chestnuts
2 cups milk
½ cup sugar
½ cup water
½ teaspoon vanilla
1 tablespoon butter
Dash salt

Whipped Cream
1 cup heavy cream
½ teaspoon vanilla or to taste
Sugar to taste

With a sharp knife, make a cut on the flat side of each chestnut. Boil in water for about 15 minutes. Remove shells.

Scald the milk in the top of a double boiler and add the peeled chestnuts. Cook in the top of the double boiler for about 30 minutes, or until very soft.

Make a syrup from the sugar and water. Cook until the syrup has reduced somewhat. When the chestnuts are done, add them to the syrup and cook for a few minutes more.

Let the chestnuts cool slightly, then add the vanilla, and put them through a food mill. Mix the butter and salt into the puree.

Mold the puree into a pair of breasts. Beat the cream until very stiff; mix it with the vanilla and sweeten to taste. Using a pastry bag with a #22 tube, pipe out a French bra on the underside of the breasts. You can decorate the bra with glacé cherries and buttercream leaves—it's so pretty! Put a small dollop of cream on top of each breast for nipples. Or a piece of chestnut or a maraschino cherry. Or, best of all, chocolate cherries with stems!

Wait until you taste this one!

Every queen we've ever known—from Cleopatra to Quentin—has at one time carried a torch, and that sparked off this dessert idea:

Flaming Queens
(Serves 4)

4 very firm bananas	**16 kumquats**
4 tablespoons butter	**½ cup sugar**
4 tablespoons lemon juice	**¼ cup dark rum**

Peel and slice the bananas in half lengthwise. Melt the butter in a heavy frying pan; place the bananas in the butter, sprinkle with lemon juice and sugar, and heat gently until the bananas turn slightly golden, about 5 minutes. Do not let them get too soft (you don't want *limp* Flaming Queens, for heaven's sakes!) Turn once or twice, very carefully, as they break easily. When almost done, put the kumquats in to warm.

When done, remove the bananas carefully to a heated serving platter, and arrange each banana half with a pair of kumquats for balls. Add rum to the sugar and lemon juice remaining in the frying pan, heat, and light. Pour flaming rum carefully over bananas and serve Queens Flaming. To squeals of delight!

Here's the most original way we ever found to get a message across, and it's one that will suit any occasion. Don't forget, "kiss" and "love" are four-letter words, too!

Four-Letter Words for the Cunning Linguist

(Makes 50 cookies)

1 cup butter
¾ cup sugar
Dash salt
1 egg
1 teaspoon vanilla

2½ cups flour
½ teaspoon baking powder
Dash nutmeg, or more to
taste

Cream the butter, sugar, and salt together. Add the egg and vanilla. Mix well. Sift the flour, baking powder, and nutmeg together. Combine the two mixtures thoroughly.

Put the dough into a cookie press, using the star-shaped tip. Since many people won't be familiar with the use of a cookie press, rather than trying to pipe out letter shapes, we suggest that you pipe out both long and short strips as needed *directly onto the cookie sheet.* Then form the letters with your fingers. Be careful—once the dough is shaped, it can't be reshaped. Put the cookie sheet into a preheated 375° F. oven and bake for 12 to 15 minutes.

Separate the words—or even the letters—with silk flowers, foil-covered candy kisses, or whatever ornament you'd like. Then spell out your words on a pretty plate or platter. (This is particularly super for Valentine's Day!)

NOTE: One of the most fun things to do with this dough is to make X's and O's and bake them. Then make a tic-tac-toe board out of colored strips of paper, foil, straws—whatever—and play cookie games in front of a Christmas fire with a big punch bowl of eggnog. It's great for family gatherings.

Here's a classic cookie everyone loves. Our recipe is a year-round best seller in The Erotic Baker®. Gingerbread Cookie People make fine holiday gifts and can even be used as place cards for a dinner party. They're so anatomically correct that all you have to do is write each person's name in icing and endow the gingerbread person accordingly!

Gingerbread Cookie People
(Makes 24 7-inch gingerbread people)

¾ cup plus 1 tablespoon shortening
1-pound box brown sugar
3 cups dark molasses
1½ tablespoons baking soda
9½ cups flour
1½ teaspoons salt
1½ teaspoons allspice
1½ teaspoons ginger

1½ teaspoons ground cloves
1½ teaspoons cinnamon
½ teaspoon ground cardamom (optional)
2 teaspoons grated orange rind (optional)
½ cup plus 1 tablespoon water

Cream the shortening and sugar together. Blend in the molasses. Sift the dry ingredients together with the spices,

and the orange rind if used, and slowly add to the creamed ingredients, alternating with the water. Chill the dough.

When the dough is well chilled, roll it out on a floured board to a thickness of between ⅛ and ¼ inch. Cut out the people using a gingerbread cookie cutter. Bake on a lightly greased cookie sheet at 425° F. for 10 to 12 minutes. Watch carefully to make sure the cookies do not burn.

~ *Decoration* ~

Royal Icing

6 cups confectioners' sugar **4 teaspoons lemon juice**
6 egg whites **Pinch of cream of tartar**

Coloring
Food coloring: *yellow*—hair; *pink*—lips, belly button, nipples; *white*—whites of eyes; *blue*—eyes and writing; *brown*—arms, breasts, and penises

Equipment
6 pastry bags **1 #5 tube: whites of eyes**
6 couplers **and blue of eyes**
1 #3 tube: writing **1 #9 tube: arms, breasts,**
1 #4 tube: mouth, belly **penises**
button, nipples **1 #48 tube: hair**

Sift the confectioners' sugar into a bowl. Beat the egg whites until thick but not stiff. Add the egg whites, lemon juice, and cream of tartar to the sugar. Stir to mix, and then beat, beat, beat! If the consistency is too soft, add more sugar; if it is too stiff, add more egg white. When it comes out of the pastry bag it should be firm but easy to work with.

Divide up the icing into 5 batches of appropriate amounts, depending on what they will be used for; that is, a small amount for the whites of eyes; a much larger amount for the brown of the arms, breasts, and penises.

Color accordingly and put each color into a pastry tube. Now, follow these simple diagrams to put the anatomical details on your fabulous Gingerbread Cookie People. Allow the icing to dry for at least 4 hours.

NOTE: Gingerbread cookie cutters can be found in any kitchen supply store.

There's a constant demand for this all-occasion cake. We've made it as a "Thank you" cake for blissful brides; we even sold a pair of them to two guys who were setting up house together; and our favorite was the one we made for a secretary who gave it to her boss with a message that read: "Can I get a raise out of this?" (We always did want to know the end of that story!) It's the one and only:

Hap-Penis Cake
(Serves 10)

For cake, jam mixture, and icing, follow instructions for Merry Widow Cake (page 113).

Cake pans
8-inch heart-shaped cake pan
1 small loaf pan, about 5 x 3½ x 2 inches (a foil pan is fine)
3 standard-size cupcake pans (again, foil is fine)

To make the cakes, follow the recipe for Merry Widow Cake (page 113). When cakes have cooled thoroughly, remove the heart-shaped cake from the pan, trim away the edges, and with a very sharp knife, level the top so that it is flat. Turn the cake over on your cake plate so that the bottom is uppermost; this will guarantee a flat top to work with.

Still working with a sharp knife, cut one end of the loaf cake back at an angle so that you can lean a cupcake, lying on its side, back against it for the head of the penis (the bottom of the cupcake is leaning against the end of the loaf cake). At the other end of the loaf, cut two sharp angles in the form of a V so that the two cupcakes that form the testicles can be leaned against either side—again, lying on their sides with their bottoms against the loaf cake. (See illustration.)

Try out the arrangement by placing the loaf cake in the center of the heart-shaped cake. Place the three cupcakes

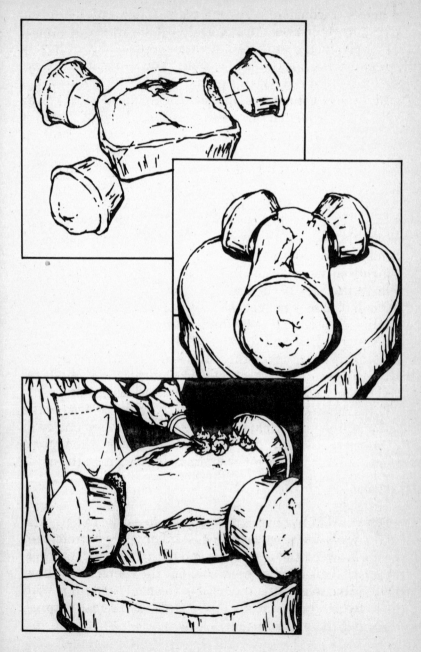

in their positions: one leaning against the front end of the loaf; the other two leaning against each of the V-shaped sides. You may want to cut the front cupcake down slightly —it depends on the size you want. You can adjust the angles in the loaf cake at this point.

Remove the cupcakes and set aside. Spread most of the jam mixture over the heart-shaped cake, leaving some for the cupcakes. Make the Buttercream Icing (either pink or mocha) as instructed on page 114. Fill a pastry bag that has a #22 tube with buttercream (don't overfill, as it makes it hard to work the bag) and make stars all over the sides and top of the cake, following the shape of the cake.

Now center the loaf cake on the heart-shaped cake. Then center the loaf on the larger cake. Place the cupcake that forms the head of the penis in place.

Position the two remaining cupcakes against the angled sides of the back of the loaf cake. Now brush the remaining jam mixture lightly over the cupcakes.

Fill the pastry bag with more buttercream and, making wavy stripes, cover the shaft of the penis. Then, using a circular motion, cover the cupcakes one by one, making wavy stripes around each cupcake until it is completely covered. If you prefer, you can cover them with stars.

Once the cake is iced, press a cherry onto the head of the penis; if it's mocha icing, try a chocolate-covered cherry or a chocolate kiss. Or, if it's that kind of an occasion, put a dollop of whipped cream or white buttercream on the head.

Enjoy, whatever the occasion!

NOTE: For a variation, cut the loaf cake in half sideways and spread either custard or white buttercream between the two layers and put them back together. Using an apple corer, core out the center of the cupcake that forms the head of the penis and fill it with white buttercream or custard—it's a real surprise when you cut into it!

A long time ago—well, not that long ago—the term "cream puff" was used to mean that someone was a wimp, spineless. But not our cream puff: he's big, virile, and tastes just wonderful.

A-Hard-Man-Is-Good-to-Find Cream Puff
(Serves 6 to 8)

1 cup water	**4 eggs**
½ cup butter	**Strawberry or coffee ice**
¼ teaspoon salt	**cream**
1 cup flour	

Bring the water, butter, and salt to a boil. Stir in the flour and, over low heat, continue stirring vigorously until the mixture pulls away from the sides of the saucepan and forms a stiff mass. Remove from the heat and cool slightly.

Preheat the oven to 450° F. Add the eggs one at a time, beating vigorously after each addition. After the last egg is thoroughly beaten in, grease a cookie sheet. Fill a cookie press or a pastry bag, using a #31 tube; holding the tube at a slant, make three strips with two thirds of the dough. Place two strips side by side; center the third strip on top.

With the remaining third of the dough, with either the pastry bag or a tablespoon, make two egg shapes for testicles, positioning them at one end of the shaft. At the other end, make one round shape for the head.

Bake at 450° F. for 15 minutes. Then reduce the heat to 325° F. and bake for 20 minutes more.

Let the cream puff cool; then cut in half lengthwise and fill with strawberry or coffee ice cream or with banana or vanilla custard.

When the cream puff is filled, serve with chocolate sauce or thawed frozen strawberries, depending on the ice cream.

NOTE: You can also fill the cream puff with banana or vanilla custard.

This, strictly speaking, is not a recipe. *But* it's the best-looking cat-o'-nine-tails you've ever seen! It's ideal for a really good-natured sadist to whip his or her favorite masochist as sweetly as possible!

Licorice Whips

9 3-foot strings red or black licorice

5-inch candy stick (cellophane wrapper left on)

8-foot length thick black yarn

Several brightly colored feathers

Line up the ends of the licorice so that they are even. Place the candy stick so that it is also lined up with the licorice ends. Tie the yarn to the end of the candy stick, wind it once around the stick and the licorice, and knot it. Carefully wind the yarn down the length of the candy stick, together with the licorice, keeping the yarn as even and tight as possible until the stick is completely covered. Knot the yarn. This is your handle.

Secure the feathers to the end of the handle by winding the yarn around enough of the feathers' length to hold them firmly in place. Wind the yarn again going down the length of the handle, this time around the feathers, candy stick, and licorice. Knot the yarn well and trim the loose ends.

This is one of the world's most *original* party favors.

This cake's one of The Erotic Baker®'s most popular desserts. It's in the best tradition of the Naughty Nineties: a high-kicking, giggling, brazen:

Merry Widow Cake
(Serves 10)

Cake
½ cup shortening
1½ cups sugar
2 eggs
2⅔ cups flour
1 tablespoon plus 1
   teaspoon baking powder
½ teaspoon salt
1 cup milk
1 teaspoon vanilla

Cake Pans
8-inch heart-shaped cake
   pan
2 4½ x 1¼-inch tart pans
   (foil pans will be fine)
2 standard size cupcake
   pans (foil pans will also
   do here)

Jam Mixture
½ cup raspberry,
   strawberry, or apricot jam
¼ teaspoon lemon juice

Buttercream Icing (see
   Note, page 116)
1 cup butter, softened
½ cup vegetable shortening
6 cups confectioners' sugar
¼ cup milk
1 tablespoon vanilla
Pink food coloring

Mocha Buttercream Icing
1 cup butter, softened
½ cup vegetable shortening
5½ cups confectioners'
   sugar
½ cup cocoa
¼ cup strong coffee

The Cake

Cream the shortening. Gradually add the sugar until the two are well blended, then blend in the eggs. Sift the flour, baking powder, and salt together. Add the dry ingredients alternately with the milk to the shortening mixture until all are incorporated. Add the vanilla and beat well.

Fill the cake pan, tart pans, and cupcake pans half to three quarters full. Bake at 375° F. for 25 to 30 minutes until well browned on top. Remove from the oven and cool thoroughly.

Decoration:

Remove the heart-shaped cake from the pan. Trim away the edges. With a very sharp knife, level the top so that it is flat. Turn the cake over on a cake plate so that the bottom is uppermost; this will guarantee a flat top to work with.

Remove the tart cakes and follow the same procedure in trimming the edges and cutting them flat. Place the two small cakes, also bottom side up, on the two rounded parts of the top of the heart cake. Now trim the edges off the cupcakes to round them, and cut off a little from the bottom of each cupcake. Place each cupcake, rounded side up, in the center of each tart shape. This will show you the final positioning of the cake parts. Now remove the cupcakes and tart shapes and set aside.

Mix the jam and lemon juice. Spread most of the jam mixture over the top of the heart-shaped cake, leaving a little for the tops of the tarts.

For *pink buttercream icing:* Mix the butter and shortening together until creamy. Gradually add the sugar and the milk. The icing should be reasonably firm. Since this depends on the amount of humidity in the air, add the liquid cautiously until the icing reaches the consistency you desire. Then, add the vanilla and a few drops of pink food coloring. If you are making *mocha buttercream icing*, mix the butter and shortening together until creamy, then sift the cocoa and confectioners' sugar together. Gradually add the sugar mixture and coffee.

Beat the buttercream as much as possible! Although we always use real butter in our frostings at The Erotic Baker®, it is necessary to use some vegetable shortening to lighten the frosting for decorating—it should be as fluffy as possible. So you want to beat in as much air as you can.

Fill a pastry bag that has a #22 tube with the buttercream (don't overfill, as it makes it hard to work the bag) and

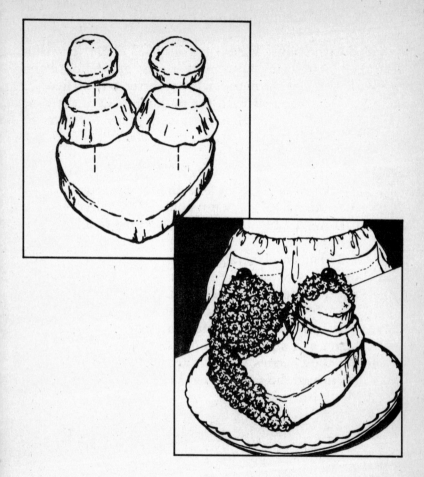

make stars all over the sides and top of the cake, following the shape of the cake. Once it is covered, place the small cakes in place where they were before, at the top of the heart. Spread the tops with the remaining jam mixture. Then center the cupcakes on top of each.

Fill the pastry bag with more buttercream and, using a circular motion, cover the tart cakes and cupcakes with buttercream stars until you have big, luscious pink or mocha breasts. Use either cherries or strawberries for nipples—or with mocha frosting, chocolate-covered cherries or chocolate kisses.

Added Attractions: Make a bra out of M & Ms, jelly candies, cinnamon drops, spearmint leaves, or whatever you think of. Or make a merry widow corset out of licorice lacing—red looks great with the pink icing. Or dress your Merry Widow any way that takes your fancy—she's a lot more fun to play with than paper dolls. Happy baking!

 NOTE: 1. If you are very handy with a pastry bag, you can make about one third more buttercream than the recipe calls for, and use it to decorate the cake with a buttercream bra, flowers, or a butterfly tattoo.

2. For an elaborate touch, core out the cupcake centers with an apple corer and fill them with either white buttercream or custard.

3. You can even have color-coordinated guests with this cake. The night a banker was guest of honor at a dinner, we demurely asked him to pluck out the cherries with his teeth—it was wonderful! He turned the same color as the icing!

When we have people around who just want something sweet to nibble on—in the way of food, that is—or when we want to serve a small, sweet, finger dessert along with fruit or ice cream, we've found these the perfect solution. In fact, we usually end up wishing we'd doubled or trebled the recipe because they vanish into thin air as soon as we serve them.

Nipple Noshes
(Makes 12)

2 egg whites
Dash salt
½ cup sugar
1 teaspoon vanilla

7-ounce package grated
   coconut
Chocolate bits

Preheat the oven to 350° F.

Beat the egg whites with salt until slightly stiff, then gradually add the sugar until the whites form very stiff peaks. Fold in the vanilla and coconut. Grease a cookie sheet well, then flour it, so that the meringues won't stick. Drop the meringues by the spoonful onto the sheet, heaping them up and rounding them as best you can. Top each one with a chocolate bit for a nipple. Bake for about 15 minutes until slightly browned.

This recipe is lovely from every point of view—it looks beautiful, smells heavenly, and tastes divine! It's the perfect dessert for that very special dinner.

Actually, a word of warning—it's also tactile! We strongly suggest that you make these the day before. The last time Karen made them, by the time she was done, Karen, the kitchen, and the cat had more chocolate on them than the cakes. (On the other hand, you could save the actual decorating until after dinner, if you want, when you could *both* decorate and help lick the chocolate off each other. . . .)

Petits Foreplay
(Makes 8 cakes)

2 cups cake flour
3 teaspoons baking powder
¼ pound butter
1 cup sugar
1 cup milk
1 teaspoon vanilla
Dash salt
3 egg whites
Mocha Buttercream (see page 113)
Raspberry jam

Icing
12 ounces milk chocolate
4 tablespoons salad oil

Decoration
Chocolate hearts in red foil
Crystallized rose or violet leaves
Green Buttercream (see Note 2, p. 119)
Raspberry jam

Utensils
8-inch square cake pan
Heart-shaped cookie cutter

Preheat the oven to 350° F. Sift the flour and baking powder together. Cream the butter and sugar. Add the dry ingredients alternately with the milk to the butter/sugar mixture. Mix in the vanilla. Adding the salt, beat the egg whites until stiff. Fold the whites into the batter.

Grease and flour the cake pan. Bake for 45 minutes or

until browned. Let the cake cool, remove from the pan, and place in the refrigerator so that it is very cold when you cut it. Using the heart-shaped cookie cutter, cut out the petits fours. Slice each one in half, making two layers, and spread the bottom layer with Mocha Buttercream. Replace the top layer and spread the top with raspberry jam.

For the icing, melt the chocolate in the top of a double boiler over simmering water (do not let it boil). Mix in the salad oil. Place the petits fours on a wire rack with a pan underneath. Pour the chocolate over each cake, adding chocolate to fill in any imperfections. Cool on waxed paper.

When cool, the cakes may be decorated in the following ways:

1. In the center of each heart, place a chocolate heart in red foil.

2. Put two crystallized rose petals on top of the heart, with Green Buttercream leaves below them (use a #67 pastry tube for forming leaves).

3. Use crystallized violets instead of roses with the Green Buttercream leaves.

4. Put a spoonful of raspberry jam in the center of the rose petals, or just use a dollop of raspberry jam without the rose petals, but with the green leaves.

NOTE: 1. This can also be made in a 9 x 12-inch baking pan, so that you have more small cakes but in only one layer. Experiment with other flavor jams —apricot is very good.

2. For Green Buttercream, follow recipe on page 114, substituting green food coloring for pink.

Pinch me, is this real? This is so-o-o luscious-looking, so voluptuous, that you want to both eat it and keep it to look at! But like all good things, this won't keep, so eat it very slowly; roll it over your tongue, lasciviously; savor each separate flavor as you come to it.

Pinch-Me Parfait
(Serves 1)

Chocolate ice cream
Chocolate sauce or syrup
Maple, chocolate-chip,
   coffee, vanilla ice creams
   (choose any 2)
Kahlua (or liqueur of
   choice)

Strawberry ice cream
Frozen strawberries or
   raspberries, thawed
Whipped cream
Maraschino cherry

At the bottom of a tall-stemmed glass, put a scoop of chocolate ice cream. Pour chocolate sauce or syrup over the ice cream. On top of the sauce, layer any two of your favorite ice creams—except that one of them should be maple—and pour a jigger of Kahlua over that. Top with a scoop of strawberry ice cream.

Pour the thawed fruit over the top. Mound whipped cream on top of that so that it comes to a peak, and on the very top place a cherry.

We wouldn't suggest mentioning this recipe to your maiden aunt—she's sure to misunderstand. They don't meow, they aren't soft and fluffy, and they don't catch mice. But they sure are cute!

Prune Pussies I

Prunes (as many as needed)
Peanut butter

Put the prunes in a pot, barely cover with water, and simmer for 20 or 30 minutes. Remove from the flame, cover, and let cool.

Slit each cooled prune, remove the pit, and stuff with peanut butter. If you're making these while company's around, you can pause every now and then and let someone lick the peanut butter off your fingers. Then continue. If you can.

Prune Pussies II

Prepare the prunes as above, but instead of stuffing them with peanut butter, mix a few drops of pink food coloring into cream cheese and stuff with that. (This is as finger-lickable as peanut butter.)

If it's Prune Whip, it must be a sadist's delight. And it's delicate, light, and fluffy, so it's an ideal victim. But who'd have the heart to attack it? We would, that's who, because it's so delicious you can't leave it alone!

Prune Whip
(Serves 4)

½ pound pitted or 1 pound unpitted prunes
3 tablespoons sugar

1 tablespoon lemon juice
Dash salt
4 egg whites

Cover the prunes with water and cook for about 20 minutes until soft. If unpitted, pit the prunes. Purée in a blender with a little of the prune liquid. You should have about 1 cup of puree.

Preheat oven to 325° F. Stir the sugar, lemon juice, and salt into the puree. Beat the egg whites until stiff. Carefully fold the prune mixture into the whites. Grease a soufflé or baking dish and gently pour the mixture into the dish. Bake for 25 to 30 minutes. Serve warm.

It's one of those lazy Saturday nights; there's nothing special planned, nowhere you feel like going, so why not try putting this dessert together. It not only tastes really good, but it'll give you ideas of how to spend Saturday night in a, please forgive the pun, fruitful manner!

Saturday Night Sundae
(Serves 1)

1 very firm ripe banana	Whipped cream
3 canned pineapple rings	Coconut
2 scoops of your favorite ice cream	1 maraschino cherry

Peel the banana. Stack the pineapple rings on top of each other. Slice the bottom of the banana so that it will stand straight. Scoop out a little indentation in the rounded end for the cherry. Stand the banana upright in the center of the stacked rings. Put 1 scoop of ice cream on each side of the banana. Put a dollop of whipped cream in the hollow in the top of the banana and stick the cherry on top. Pile whipped cream around the ice cream and sprinkle with coconut. (If you want a really jazzy effect, tint the coconut any color you'd like to go with the color of the ice cream.)

NOTE: For a salad variation, see Big Boy Banana (page 79).

Next time you have a party, try these melt-in-your-mouth cookies. Ask your friends which part they prefer when you pass them around—there's one for each taste!

Spare Parts Sugar Cookies
(Makes 18 to 20 cookies)

2¼ cups flour
¼ teaspoon salt
2 teaspoons baking powder
½ cup shortening
1 cup sugar
2 eggs, beaten
½ teaspoon vanilla
1 teaspoon grated lemon
  rind

1 tablespoon milk
Food coloring as desired
Maraschino cherries, cut in
  quarters
Additional sugar
Red food coloring

Sift the dry ingredients together. Cream the shortening, sugar, eggs, vanilla, and lemon rind. Add the dry ingredients and milk to the creamed mixture. Add food coloring or leave plain.

Preheat the oven to 375° F. Cut out the breasts with either the edge of a glass or a round cookie cutter. Overlap two circles, according to the illustration, and press the overlapping edges firmly together. Make a pattern for the penis (see illustration), and cut out the dough to shape. Add red food coloring to some sugar. Sprinkle the head of the penis with the red sugar, and make red nipples in the center of the breasts. In the middle of each nipple, put one quarter of a cherry. Bake for 12 minutes.

Some like tits, some like ass—with this recipe you have the best of all possible worlds, because you get both.

Tits and Ass Mousse
(Serves 4)

1 package gelatin	4 eggs, separated
¼ cup cold water	4 teaspoons sugar
½ cup boiling water	1 tablespoon rum
1 tablespoon instant coffee	Chocolate morsels

Pour the gelatin into the cold water. Let sit for a few minutes. Combine the gelatin with the boiling water and boil gently until dissolved. Remove from the flame and let cool.

Stir instant coffee into the egg yolks and let sit to dissolve the coffee while you beat the egg whites. Beat whites until very stiff. Set aside.

Add the sugar to the coffee/egg yolk mixture and beat until foamy. Add the rum and beat again. Stir in the cooled gelatin, then carefully fold in the egg whites so that the mixture stays light and foamy.

Breasts: Spoon some of the mixture into two small bowls and put into the refrigerator for about 20 to 30 minutes, just long enough to set very slightly. Remove at this point; you will find the whites and liquid have separated. Beat again well with the egg beater and return to the refrigerator for at least an hour, until the mousse is set but is not too hard.

When thoroughly chilled, run a knife around the inside edge and dip briefly into a bowl of hot water. Invert on a serving plate and add chocolate morsel nipples.

Ass: Pour the remaining mixture into a bowl just large enough to hold it and follow directions for Breasts.

When thoroughly chilled, run a knife around the edge of the bowl to separate the mousse from the bowl. You can also dip the bowl briefly into a larger bowl of hot water to loosen the mousse. Put the serving plate you wish to use over the bowl and invert. Shake slightly (you may have to dip again, if necessary, but don't overdo it) until the mousse separates from the bowl and goes onto the plate. At this point, using a large tablespoon and a knife, you can easily sculpt the mousse into a really cute little brown derriere. With the knife, cut down the center two thirds of the way, making the separation, and round the edges with the tablespoon. Work fairly quickly so that the mousse doesn't get too warm. Return to the refrigerator for several hours until firmly set. You can prepare this and leave it overnight—perfect for a no-work dinner party dessert.

We do all sorts of cute understated decorations with this one. Try putting one chocolate morsel in the middle of one buttock, point pushed in—it makes a great beauty mark! Or make whipped cream bikini panties. You can edge them with coconut if you like.

If you make whipped cream bikinis, be sure to make a whipped cream bra for the breasts. What the well-dressed Tits and Ass Mousse is wearing this season!

NOTE: When the mousse is inverted, it may be covered with a film of the dark coffee. Either leave it, if you like, or scrape it off gently with a knife—it comes off very easily.

It's Halloween, and we are about to give you a recipe for the most delicious chocolate cake and the sexiest witch you've ever eaten (oops!) or seen. It's pure magic! Feed it to anyone you want to bewitch, and they'll be yours forever.

Witch's Tit Cake
(Serves 10)

Cake
2 squares semisweet
   chocolate
1 cup milk, divided
1 cup sugar
¼ cup butter
1 egg, separated
1 cup flour
1 teaspoon baking soda
Dash salt
¼ teaspoon vanilla or
   almond flavoring

Cooking Utensils
9-inch heart-shaped cake
   pan
2 3-inch bowls

Decoration
Buttercream Icing (page
   114), substituting yellow
   and red food coloring for
   pink
Chocolate or coffee ice
   cream
Whipped cream
Candy corn
Chocolate syrup *or* licorice
   laces, for lacing
Any Halloween candies
   that take your fancy

Melt the chocolate in ½ cup of the milk and cook slowly until thick. Add the sugar and butter and continue cooking slowly while mixing until dissolved. Remove from the heat and let cool.

Preheat the oven to 300° F. Beat the egg white until stiff. Beat the yolk well and add to the cooled chocolate mixture. Sift together the flour, baking soda, and salt, and stir into the mixture. Stir in the remaining milk and the flavoring. Fold in the egg white.

Grease and flour the cake pan; pour in the batter and bake for 50 minutes. Remove from the oven and let cool.

Decoration: Soften the ice cream. Line the two bowls with plastic wrap and pack them tightly with the softened ice cream. Put into the freezer and freeze solid.

Remove the cake from the pan. Trim away the edges. With a very sharp knife, level the top so that it is flat. Turn the cake over on the cake plate so that the bottom is uppermost; this will guarantee a flat top to work with.

Prepare the Buttercream Icing following the instructions on page 114, mixing yellow and red food coloring to make a good Halloween orange. Ice the cool cake with the buttercream, using a hot, wet spatula to create a flat surface.

The remaining decoration will have to be done quickly just before the cake is served. Dip the bowls with the ice cream quickly into hot water and turn them out upside down onto the two rounded parts at the top of the heart. Working quickly, make a whipped cream half-bra around each ice cream breast, and put a dollop of whipped cream at each nipple. Stick a candy corn into the center of each nipple or use the little pumpkin-shaped candies.

You can decorate the rest of the cake in a number of ways. We like to outline a corset under the breasts with whipped cream from a pastry tube. Then we stick candy corn upright at regular intervals in the whipped cream for hooks. We either drizzle chocolate syrup or sauce between the candy corn to make the lacing, or you can use licorice laces instead. And on the plate around the bottom edge of the entire cake, we pipe a decorative edging of whipped cream and put Halloween candies here and there.

NOTES: 1. Instead of making a bra of whipped cream, you can also make one of chocolate by sticking chocolate morsels into the bottom half of the breasts, points into the ice cream and edges touching. It gives the effect of a lacy brown bra. And it tastes awfully good with coffee ice cream.

2. If you want to use this recipe for a two-layer cake, double the ingredients. It works perfectly.

LOVE ELIXIRS

The Erotic Bakers are not teetotalers, so they know about drinks. Alcohol is excellent for a little excitement, for relaxation, and like a good striptease artist, for removing those last inhibitions. But if it's overdone, it can send you—or him, or her, or them—straight to bed to sleep, wasting all your good preparations. (No, we didn't mean good intentions!)

This is a cautionary note, because the drinks that follow are so good, and so harmless-tasting, that sometimes they get tossed off like lemonade. They're not!

Now that we've put in our note of warning, mix, drink, and above all, enjoy!

This is too heavenly for words—so we won't say anything. Just try one!

Angel's Tits
(Makes 1)

Crème de cacao
Heavy cream

Maraschino cherries

Fill a very small brandy snifter two thirds full with crème de cacao. Carefully float a layer of heavy cream on top by pouring over the back of a spoon, taking care the two don't mix. Run a toothpick through a maraschino cherry so that the cherry is in the middle of the toothpick. Balance the toothpick across the middle of the glass so the cherry is centered over the cream.

We're told that this drink was originally called a French 75, after a big gun used in World War I, because of the wallop it packed. Well, with that kind of kick, what could be better for our nefarious purposes than a:

French 69
(Makes 1)

1 jigger brandy
½ teaspoon sugar
Squirt of lemon juice

Squirt of orange juice
8 ounces champagne

Put the brandy in the bottom of a 12-ounce glass. Stir in the sugar and add the lemon and orange juices to taste. Fill the glass with champagne. And watch out!

This is great for clearing the cobwebs out of your eyes and getting you moving! If you have a tulip-shaped glass, this is just made for serving a blushing:

Gay Grapefruit
(Makes 1)

Pink grapefruit juice   **Vodka**

Mix grapefruit juice and vodka in proportions desired, and drink!

These two are great drinks after playing in the snow, sitting through an ice hockey or football game, or for any winter celebration. Highly recommended!

Hot and Steamy Mulled Wine
(For 4)

1 liter Lambrusco   **4 orange slices, divided**
2 tablespoons honey   **1 ounce vodka per glass**
3 cinnamon sticks   **(optional)**
½ cup raisins

Heat the wine, honey, cinnamon sticks, raisins, and 2 orange slices until steaming. *Do not boil*. If using vodka, put it in glass mugs or cappuccino glasses. Trim each glass with half an orange slice and pour in the steamy wine.

Hot, Steamy, and Spicy Mulled Wine
(For 4)

1 liter Rhine wine	½ cup golden raisins
2 tablespoons honey	3 cinnamon sticks
6 cloves	¼ teaspoon nutmeg

Heat the wine, honey, cloves, raisins, and cinnamon sticks until steaming. *Do not boil.* Pour into glass mugs or cappuccino glasses. Sprinkle each with a dash of nutmeg.

Here's a drink for those early days—it still blushes!

Lovers' Lemonade

3 crushed strawberries	Lemonade (frozen or fresh)
1½ ounces vodka	1 slice lemon
Dash grenadine	

Put the strawberries in the bottom of a 12-ounce glass. Add the vodka and grenadine and fill the glass with lemonade. Add ice cubes and stir. Serve with a slice of lemon and two straws.

This is for one of those mornings: either a Morning After the Night Before; or a cold, rainy day when nobody wants to go outside; or a snowy winter morning when you'd just like to have a pick-me-up and get back in bed and snuggle.

It's warm and aromatic and evokes coziness and affection —which I suppose is why we called it:

Loving Cup
(Makes 1)

½ cup French roast or Colombian mocha coffee
½ cup hot chocolate

1 ounce cognac
Dash cinnamon or nutmeg

The coffee should be strong and the hot chocolate should be very rich, ideally made with half-and-half. Mix in a proportion of 1 part hot coffee to 1 part hot chocolate and stir in the cognac.

Serve in mugs or long-stemmed glasses (pour it over a spoon in the case of glasses to avoid cracking the glass). Sprinkle with cinnamon or nutmeg. Yummy!

This is one of the perfect endings to a meal—or to have as a nightcap, especially if you are about to go out on the prowl!

Pussy Café

Pour very hot espresso or strong black coffee into cups. Then float Irish Cream Liqueur on top.

This is a sultry lady who packs quite a punch!

Tropical Trollop

1 ounce light rum
1 ounce dark rum
2 to 3 ounces pineapple
   juice
Juice of ½ lemon
2 ounces orange juice

1 teaspoon superfine sugar
Dash grenadine
Pineapple stick
Orange slice
Maraschino cherry

Shake all the ingredients together with ice. Garnish with a fresh pineapple stick, a slice of orange, and a cherry.

There are traditional aphrodisiacs, and there are personal aphrodisiacs. What makes this drink The Erotic Baker®'s own special brew is that it has three of *our* favorite aphrodisiacs: nutmeg, honey, and of course, champagne! Try this, and you won't need a broomstick to fly.

Witch's Brew
(Serves 25)

¾ cup honey
1 quart brandy
6 bottles champagne
6 bottles sparkling water

Dash nutmeg
1 package frozen melon
   balls

Drizzle honey around the sides of a large punch bowl, then pour the liquids in the bowl and mix. Grate as much nutmeg as you want to cover the top. Float the melon balls in the punch. Fly.

Teetotaler's Tipples

This is a surprising pick-me-up. It's cool, refreshing, and unexpectedly different.

Ruth's Titillating Tea

Pink lemonade   **Iced tea**

Mix to taste, add lots of ice—a sprig of mint, if you like —and enjoy!

For the blushing bride, for the vanishing virgins, we give you:

Virgin Mary

Tomato juice   **Dash Tabasco**
Worcestershire sauce   **Salt**
Lemon juice   **Freshly ground pepper**

To chilled tomato juice, add ingredients as desired to taste.

EROTIC
ENTERTAINING

We've given you some of our favorite recipes, and now it's time to think about how to put them together. It's fantasy time!

Adults and kids are the same when it comes to having parties. They both like to have fun. It's just a different kind of fun. But the excitement's the same. So if you're planning a party, let your imagination go to work and think of what kind of fantasy you'd like your party to express.

Even simpler, when a special friend—or several friends—are coming over to eat, have fun beforehand deciding which erotic dishes go with whom; which dishes go with which; what drink will underline either the Appeteaser or the dessert; which recipes will get the message across (like A-Hard-Man-Is-Good-to-Find Cream Puff?).

We've given you a wide range of shaped dishes, dishes with double-entendre names, and dishes with wonderfully sensuous textures and tastes. You're getting into the habit of looking at food in a different way—as sensuous, sexy, and erotic. Now, show your friends.

We've put together a group of menus in detail just to give you an idea how we'd do it. Then we've given you some outline suggestions for other ideas. Before long, you'll be out on your own, thinking up your individual fabulous party menus. And that'll be even better. Because they express you!

Bridal Shower
Buffet

Last time we gave a bridal shower, we went all out. This is how we did it, and you can take it from here.

First of all, instead of a tablecloth, we used a beautiful cream-colored satin sheet to cover the table. At the head of the table, we put two pillows with pillowcases to match. That was the bed. Next to the head of the table, we put a low coffee table with a lovely, fresh bouquet of fragile spring flowers in the center. Around it, we piled the shower gifts.

Our buffet started off with Virgin Marys; those who wanted to, added vodka.

Along with the Virgin Marys, we served Rosy Nipples as an Appeteaser—the colors all looked wonderful against the cream-colored sheet! Besides, red caviar seemed like the right festive touch for the occasion.

After Rosy Nipples, Blushing Boobs and Suspended Animation Salad make the perfect shower dish. And along with it, we served two loaves of bread—His and Her. To keep up the theme, we used the smallest scoop we could find and made little butter breasts to go along with the bread. We topped the butter with red caviar nipples, too—but you can also use inexpensive domestic black caviar or capers, if you like.

We served two desserts for this party: On her side of the bed we put Chastity Chest-nut Puree; on his side, we put a big, beautiful Hap-Penis Cake. Though come to think of it, by then they should have both been on the same side of the bed!

Anyhow, that was *our* Bridal Shower Buffet, and it was a great success. You can also choose among Cock-Teasers or Beefy Parts; if you want a hot main dish, there's Party Parts or Eve's Temptation; for vegetables, Virgin's Delight or Coy Cauliflower; and for dessert, for a lark, make up lots of Four-Letter Words cookies and let your guests play Four-Letter Words—or maybe change it to Three-Letter Words this time—that way you can get from "coy" and "shy" to "hot" in no time flat!

Fourth of July Bang! Picnic

Picnics are something we always love. A picnic is special, both erotic *and* romantic. Our favorite way of picnicking is with a loaf of bread, a bottle of chilled white wine, Thou—and a salad. When we want a really special touch, we take good crystal to drink out of, a favorite tablecloth to eat on, and silver tableware. If you really want to be dashing, add a small vase with a tiny bunch of flowers—or a single favorite—to put in the middle of the cloth.

Of course, the Fourth of July has always been the traditional picnic time in America. Let's hope it's a hot, sunny day. The kind of day that's already erotic because of the heat and the feel of the sun on your body and the summer smells in the air. Put a bottle of white wine in the refrigerator the night before to make sure it's well chilled. (If you prefer red wine, and it's a hot day, chill it a bit before you leave so it won't be too warm later.) We put a couple of plastic bags of ice cubes in a plastic or Styrofoam bucket and keep the wine in that. It's a super place to keep butter in, too, if you're taking some along.

There are lots of dishes in the book that are perfect for a picnic. Any of the molded salads (we don't advise chicken liver in the heat, however), or a couple of Amorous Avocados, Cock-Teasers, Pussy Pita, or Blushing Boobs. A loaf of

His or Her Bread is a must, and we usually take along a side salad of carrot curls and raisins (made exactly like it sounds —curls of raw carrot mixed with raisins and salad dressing), and a dessert as simple as Gingerbread Cookie People. If you don't want wine, try a thermos of Lover's Lemonade, or Ruth's Titillating Tea.

Now take your hamper either out to the country or to the concert in the park, or wherever they're showing fireworks. We might point out, though, that with this picnic, you can make your own fireworks. So be sure to find a secluded spot!

A Romantic Dinner for Two

What could be more important than an intimate Romantic Dinner for Two? It's the best way to celebrate something special between two special people—anything from a first dinner together to an anniversary, or a special time like a birthday or New Year's Eve. It's for the first week you meet that important person, or for celebrating the tenth year you've spent together—or, if you're very lucky, the twenty-fifth anniversary!

This dinner for two should be formal, yet relaxed and pleasing to every sense. Use your best linen and silver and crystal. If you don't have wonderful china, you can go to your local party store and buy deep purple paper plates with napkins to match—or any other color that is sensuously arousing. We use warm peach or pink, for instance, because it looks fabulous with brass candleholders. If you don't have crystal, maybe this is the time to go out and splurge on two beautiful glasses—they'll never go to waste!

Buy lots and lots of gorgeous colored candles to go with your linen and/or plates. And if you have a fireplace, build a fire! But even if you don't, keep the lights down low.

There should be music playing softly in the background. Choose your program well in advance of the evening, the kind of music you both love. It doesn't matter if it's fifteenth-century lute or 1920s jazz. It's what the two of you care about that's important. If your budget allows it, you might check out a restaurant that has a pianist or violinist and see how much they'd charge to come play for a couple of hours. Extravagant? Yes, but wonderfully romantic—and totally erotic!

One tall red rose in a crystal or silver vase is a perfect touch. If you don't have a slim, elegant vase, then use a tall, slim wine bottle—it'll look every bit as good. Or try an orchid, that most erotic of flowers; they come in amazing colors. Of course, in the right frame of mind, even daisies in a warm, earthy brown teapot are erotic.

This dinner should begin the evening you've always dreamed about—warm, intimate, sensual. But for it to happen, here are a few practical hints.

1. Run through or list everything you have to do several days before the evening of the dinner. This is a good time to program your music.

2. Buy whatever you can in advance, and if you have many things to get the day of the dinner, have them delivered. Otherwise, once dinner is cooked you'll be so tired you'll just want to go to sleep.

3. Find a good cheese store and make a careful selection of cheeses. Otherwise, skip the cheese course.

4. Choose a very good white wine—Graves, Pouilly-Fuissé, Pouilly-Fumé—and make sure it's well chilled for the evening.

We'd begin the evening with the white wine and Passion Pâté, softly shaped into luscious, erotic mounds. With the pâté, serve tiny, tart cornichon pickles. Then, on a lighter note (you're actually orchestrating this dinner), continue with Frogs Legs' Follies dancing across their plates, accompanied by Pommes de Terre Pudeur and Simple But Sensuous String Beans. A simple salad can be served either with the main course or immediately after. Then comes a selection—it can be very small but very choice—of the fine French cheeses you went to a lot of trouble to find: tangy goat's cheese, creamy Brie, sharp Bleu, whatever took your fancy.

After the meal, settle down in front of the fireplace (or on the couch or on pillows on the floor) with a silver tray holding The Erotic Baker®'s very favorite champagne, Veuve Cliquot, with Petits-Foreplay. (If you don't have a silver tray, any small, inexpensive tray can be covered with a beautiful napkin, or one of those special-color napkins you bought at the party store.) Rich with chocolate, delicious in taste, these special petits-four are topped with either crystallized flower petals or small foil-wrapped chocolate hearts. Hearts on hearts—what better symbol of the evening as you slowly feed them to each other between sips of champagne.

Later in the evening—much, much later—you can serve Pussy Café or Italian espresso with a twist of lemon in those special demitasse cups, or strong American coffee, also with a twist of lemon if you like, in your very best china cups. If you serve plain coffee, you might try along with it a fine cognac in brandy snifters that the two of you can cup between your hands, slowly rolling them back and forth, as you toast each other, gazing into each other's eyes.

Salut!

Intimate Morning After the Night Before

It was some night! We don't have to go into the details, but our Romantic Dinner for Two seems to have gone on all night (see page 145). And on . . . and on . . . and suddenly here it is, noon the next day, and we're starved!

Superman and Wonderwoman Oyster Stew. Of course. That's why it's in the book. And the joy of it is that you can crawl into the kitchen and throw it together in 10 minutes maximum. It's also healthy, hot, filling, and strengthening—just the sort of thing your mother would have made to send you to bed and off to sleep. Or, since rumor has it that oysters are indeed aphrodisiac too, maybe it'll just send you back to bed, period.

Then there's also Suspended Animation Salad, which if you'd had the foresight to anticipate last night in advance, should already be in the refrigerator ready to eat.

You might consider one of the two Morning-After Breakfasts or One-Hung-Low Eggs—look under Titillations if you want an egg-y breakfast. You might, because if it's much earlier than noon, you probably haven't gotten around to going to sleep yet.

148

His and Her Breads are already in the bread box. And we'd like to remind you that the Loving Cup in the Love Elixirs section was just made for the Morning After—with or without accompanying food.

We're leaving this menu deliberately sketchy because it's pretty difficult to set this meal up in advance. Or to know what time you'll want to eat. Or what you'll feel like eating. Or even to be sure who you'll be with.

Of course, it also could have been a disaster. In that case, all we can suggest is a big pot of black coffee and A-Hard-Man-Is-Good-to-Find Cream Puff. And better luck next time!

New Position Office Party

One of The Erotic Baker®'s biggest shocks was the discovery that one of the most popular uses of our cakes is for office parties! And for Wall Street, no less. (No wonder the Stock Market goes up and down so much—nobody's paying attention!)

So we figured we really should give some thought to office parties—why settle for just a cake! Take your lunch hour and turn that into the office party instead of the usual at-4:00-everybody-come-to-the-main-office office party.

So-o-o, make yourself a spread on somebody's desk. (No, no—that's not the kind of spread we mean; that's for after everybody's gone home.) People can be assigned various things to make a few days before—or better, pull slips from someone's paperclip box to pick who gets to make what.

We strongly suggest Mounds of Pleasure Cheese Spread. It's a natural for this kind of buffet, and it's something that *always* gets lots of giggles. Also Cock-Teasers—easy to make and easy to carry to work.

Main dishes might be something like Pussy Pita because you'll probably be having a bunch of things and won't want a real main dish. Or any of the molded salads.

Dessert's a cinch. Make either a Merry Widow Cake or a

Hap-Penis Cake and pipe the appropriate message in a contrasting color buttercream across any part you like. We have a hunch no work will get done the week before, while the whole office tries to think up appropriately kinky messages. But it'll be one office party no office will ever forget.

Halloween Masked Ball

Halloween has always been one of our favorite holidays. It's that time of year when the air is sharp and nippy; it smells faintly of woodsmoke, leaves crunch underfoot, and everything feels exciting and alive. And Halloween itself is scary and mysterious—everything hints at the forbidden, sending shivers down your spine. Masquerades and costumes and masks—time to try out different roles and surprise your partner with a whole different "you."

For Halloween itself, we always carve a big, erotic pumpkin. We buy the largest one we can find and carve a penis on one side and a vagina on the other. It's great when it glows in the dark! (Believe us, it throws a different light on things!)

We love masquerade balls, of course. Then you not only can fantasize, but can make all your fantasies come true. Which is what this whole book is about, isn't it? So, for a Halloween Masked Ball:

Use a white sheet as a tablecloth. Make faces out of fluorescent paint on the cloth, or paint erotic shapes. Put the pumpkin out on the table. Use lots of candles—black and orange ones, or even all-black ones, and one ultra violet black light to show up the fluorescent paint. The light from the pumpkin and candles and the fluorescent paint make quite an effect. We love big, black balloons, too.

Set out on the table is the obvious Appeteaser: Devilish Whores d'Oeuvres. We usually serve Teeny Weenies along with them for balance. This is also a great time to serve a platter of Vegetables in the Raw. It's a fun contest for this kind of party—and think what Halloween prizes you could give. If you do serve Vegetables in the Raw, add Tabasco to the Honey Pot Dip, which makes it a Devilish Hot Dip! And if you want, throw in a spoonful of capers for added interest and tang. Just think of all those disguised figures carefully sculpting "forbidden" objects out of vegetables—devilish male parts, witchy female parts, and all kinds of demonic combinations. Sometimes you never do get to the main course.

But if you do, we suggest either of our two main-course favorites for this: Party Parts, or something we invented especially for Halloween: Vampire Hearts. Make the Broken Hearts recipe, but instead of cutting the hearts in two, leave them whole and run a large nail through each one. The ideal thing is one of those long aluminum nails for baking potatoes. Hot Hussy 'Taters or Pecker Pudding goes well with either of these main dishes, and the Hot Hussy 'Taters are also hot and spicy.

Dessert? Witch's Tit Cake, what else? Or if you do want a "what else," we suggest any of the Ball recipes, or better, several of them mixed—and don't forget Witch's Balls. They do carry out the dismembered theme of the evening. (This is all vicarious—your guests certainly want to keep *their* members intact!)

Carry on after dinner with our own special Witch's Brew —it's special because it has three—count 'em, three—aphrodisiacs. So we do mean, carry on!

Halloween traditionally was connected with orgies. This is your Halloween Masked Ball, there are lots of people, let it go wherever it goes. We wish you a devilishly fine party!

S & M Dinner

The table's covered with a rubber sheet. There are ropes and handcuffs over the backs of the chairs. Heavy ropes and pieces of chain are hung on the walls. Some of the guests are tied to their seats or the backs of the chairs; some are handcuffed to the guest next to them—so that they have one hand free to eat with. The placemats are red western bandanas; the plates are black. Heavy glass mugs hold the drinks, and along the table are heavy, candlestick holders with black candles in them. Preferably big, fat candles. Whatever color napkins you choose—anything dark and quirky; cock rings make great napkin holders for this particular dinner. And in front of each place is a party favor— a licorice whip.

Of course the meal starts with Celery in Bondage, served with rough rye bread or Swedish hardtack. After it comes a helpless Trussed Chicken to be served up to the guests— the S's get to toss a coin to see who'll be allowed to carve it.

Some of the guests who are tied to their chairs might be served dinner on plates just a little out of their reach—for a while, at least, until someone feels sorry enough to push their plates close enough so that they can eat. Super Stud Potatoes insist on being served with the Trussed Chicken, and Coy Cauliflower goes just fine with them both.

If you want a touch of salad on the side, serve whole

cucumbers in the rough. Your guests can peel them, slice them, cut them up in chunks and either eat them salted or dipped into your choice of dressing.

For dessert, Prune Whip. And after that, there's something deliciously perverse about serving B & B with the coffee! And after *that*—well, that's up to your guests, isn't it?

A Menu Miscellany!

Free-Again Divorce Party

We don't know who did what to whom, or why, but the divorce just came through. So you've called up your closest friends to come over to celebrate—or commiserate.

We'd start off with Mounds of Pleasure Cheese Spread—after what you've been through, you need all the pleasure you can get—and we'd serve Tropical Trollops with it.

Naturally the main dish will be Cooked Goose—or it could be Broken Hearts. Whichever one suits. But either way, Cute Carrot Cocks are a must. And Hot Hussy 'Taters will do just fine, too.

Dessert could be either Blonde Bombshell Ambrosia or Numb Nuts. Then follow dessert with Pussy Café—what have you got to lose?

P.S.—We'd get bunches of brightly colored, helium-filled balloons and let them loose to bob happily around the ceiling. Tie different-colored yarns to them, and anybody who wants one can just yank on an end and pull it down. (If it was *that* kind of a divorce, you could always get dark colors.)

Bachelor's Blast, or The Last Supper

The pièce de résistance for this supper is a Sexy Surprising Salad: the Salade de Bonne Femme. It sure beats the old-fashioned girl-bursting-out-of-a cake!

Surrounding it could be Mozzarella Mammaries, Party Parts, Potent-ate Potatoes, Harem Delight, Prune Pussies . . . whatever turns you on!

Sunday Night Orgy

There are going to be lots of people, so you need something big—to feed lots of people, that is. And something that's hearty, too, for energy. We suggest a couple of large versions of Donna's Penis Pie or Rachel's Cheatin' Heart Chili. Hot and spicy!

Put out a big bowl of Tiny Tushy Vinaigrette to start things off, with a whole range of drinks—though personally, we'd start with French 69's.

This is another occasion where a Sexy Surprising Salad— or better, two—would be perfect. And to end dinner and get the night off to a great start, by all means serve Brett's Fanny Fondue. This is the evening it was invented for.

And now, as a climax, let us have a:

Happy Holiday Gala

French 69's

Passion Pâté

Love Boats ★ Suckling Duck ★ Pecker Pudding

Aunt Patrika's Pickled Prickles ★ Peel-Me-a-Grape Salad

His and Her Breads

Brandied Bottoms or Flaming Queens

Petits Foreplay

Cognac   *Espresso*

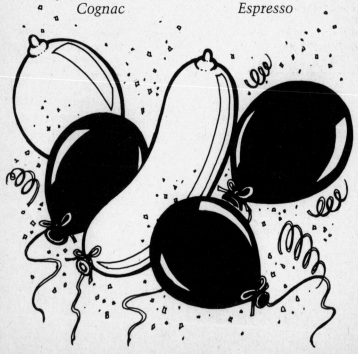

Tasty Cookbooks from PLUME

(0452)

☐ **CHINESE MEATLESS COOKING by Stella Lau Fessler.** This superb, completely authentic guide gives the historical, ethical, and nutritional background of this classic vegetarian cuisine, and offers a thorough glossary of ingredients and a list of sample menus. If you want to limit or avoid meat and experience many sublime joys of cooking and dining you'll welcome this book.   (253861—$6.95)*

☐ **CHINESE SEAFOOD COOKING by Stella Lau Fessler.** Over 130 Chinese recipes are included in this cookbook of Chinese classic cuisine; from the simplest family cooking to elaborate banquet masterpieces. You will expand both your cooking horizons and your dining enjoyment as you sample everything from seafood dishes to exotic delicacies.   (252652—$5.95)

☐ **CHINESE POULTRY COOKING by Stella Lau Fessler.** This complete guide includes hundreds of authentic, exquisite, easy-to-follow recipes from the six great schools of Chinese cooking. Also included are Chinese cooking techniques adapted for American kitchens and invaluable practical guidance in finding and choosing the best ingredients, both domestic and Chinese.   (253659—$7.95)

☐ **THE JOY OF COOKING by Irma S. Rombauer and Marion Rombauer Becker.** America's best-loved cookbook has become even better. This revised edition includes new recipes, drawings, and menus; tips on entertaining, herbs, spices, seasonings, and ingredients; plus a complete cross-referenced index cited by *Time, Saturday Evening Post,* and the *National Observer* as "first among the basic cookbooks."   (254256—$7.95)

All prices higher in Canada.

To order, use the convenient coupon on the next page.

Ⓟ

Great Recipes from PLUME

(0452)

☐ **A MOSTLY FRENCH FOOD PROCESSOR COOKBOOK by Colette Rossant and Jill Harris Herman.** A modern, time-saving adaptation of 170 traditional French recipes—from simple hors d'oeuvres to elegant entrées. With detailed illustrations and a complete evaluation of the leading 18 food processors.　(252385—$4.95)

☐ **THE LOS ANGELES TIMES CALIFORNIA COOKBOOK compiled and edited by Betsey Balsley, Food Editor and Food Staff of the *Los Angeles Times*.** More than 650 fresh, delicious and healthful recipes and menus that reflect and capture the sunny distinctiveness and ethnic diversity of California cuisine.　(254485—$9.95)

☐ **THE JEWISH LOW-CHOLESTEROL COOKBOOK by Roberta Leviton. Introduction by Rabbi Meyer J. Strassfeld. Revised edition.** Combining dishes from Europe, the Middle East, and Asia with American favorites and traditional Jewish fare, here are 375 tempting kosher recipes for healthy, hearty eating.　(254655—$7.95)

☐ **THE GOOD CAKE BOOK by Diana Dalsass.** At last, every cake lover's dream has come true. In this one deliciously readable volume are clear, concise, complete-from-beginning-to-mouth-watering-end recipes for every kind of cake you might desire—and how to make each of them in less than thirty minutes. With over 180 easy-preparation recipes.　(254493—$6.95)

All prices higher in Canada.

Buy them at your local bookstore or use this convenient
coupon for ordering.

THE NEW AMERICAN LIBRARY, INC.
P.O. Box 999, Bergenfield, New Jersey 07621

Please send me the PLUME BOOKS I have checked above. I am enclosing $_____(please add $1.50 to this order to cover postage and handling). Send check or money order—no cash or C.O.D.'s. Prices and numbers are subject to change without notice.

Name_____

Address_____

City_____State_____Zip Code_____

Allow 4-6 weeks for delivery.
This offer is subject to withdrawal without notice.

Quality Paperbacks from PLUME and MERIDIAN

(0452)

☐ **MILLER'S COURT by Arthur R. Miller.** An examination of how the law works and what it means by the well-known Harvard law professor and award-winning national TV commentator. Putting the reader in the middle of a stimulating and provocative discussion that ranges over many of the crucial issues in American life today, Miller takes you step-by-step through the complexities of the law so that you gain a clear understanding of what the consequences of one decision are for countless other cases. (253977—$6.95)

☐ **JOAN McELROY's DOLLS' HOUSE FURNITURE BOOK.** How to make every kind of miniature "house furnishing," from Early American chairs to modern sofas, refrigerators, rugs, books—even a box of chocolates and a miniature family. Her patterns are absolutely foolproof, and photographs show you what you can accomplish with everyday objects and throw-aways. (251885—$6.95)

☐ **THE FURNISH YOUR HOME BY MAIL CATALOGUE by Sarah Gallick with Mary Gallick.** Carefully arranged for quick and easy references, this definitive catalogue gives you the names, addresses, toll free phone numbers, products, price ranges, and credit card policies of firms all over America, and tells you how to acquire their lavish catalogues. (252911—$9.95)

☐ **LOS ANGELES TIMES STYLEBOOK: A Manual for Writers, Editors, Journalists and Students compiled by Frederick S. Holley.** Grammar, punctuation, the general meanings and subtle nuances of words, and a wide range of journalistic techniques are among the important language tools included in this stylebook created for and used by the staff of the *Los Angeles Times.* Alphabetically arranged for quick reference and ideal for fascinating browsing. (005523—$6.95)

All prices higher in Canada.

To order, use the convenient coupon on the next page.

Ⓟ

Great Reading from PLUME

(0452)

☐ **ORDINARY MIRACLES by Erica Jong.** The newest collection of poetry from the renowned writer and poet. The subjects of these marvelously accessible poems are pregnancy, childbirth, parenthood, divorce, death, the fear of love, and the rebirth of the spirit and the flesh that comes only when one remains open to loving. "I was much moved, elated, awed by these new poems. Here is an incredibly honest art."—Anthony Burgess   (254361—$5.95)

☐ **THE OFFICIAL M.D. HANDBOOK by Anna Eva Ricks, M.D.** The life of a doctor—from med school to malpractice insurance. A humorous account of doctors and their world.   (254388—$4.95)

☐ **NOT JUST ANOTHER PRETTY FACE: An Intimate Look at America's Top Male Models by Karen Hardy.** They are the stuff of fantasies: America's most wanted men, the top male fashion and celebrity models. But who are the *real* men beneath those glamorous, sexy exteriors? Find out all the inside details of the twenty most famous faces and bodies in the U.S. including Michael Ives, Rick Edwards and Jim Palmer in these revealing profiles. With over 100 photos.
          (253950—$11.95)

☐ **THE NAKED CIVIL SERVANT by Quentin Crisp.** In 1931, Quentin Crisp "came out" in London as a self-confessed, self-evident homosexual. His outrageous manner, flamboyant exhibitionism, and unconventional behavior shocked London society. This is his extraordinary autobiography that inspired the acclaimed TV drama. "A work of great wit, intelligence and sensitivity."—*Washington Post*
          (254132—$6.95)†

All prices higher in Canada.

† Not available in Canada

———————————————————————————————

Buy them at your local bookstore or use this convenient
coupon for ordering.

THE NEW AMERICAN LIBRARY, INC.
P.O. Box 999, Bergenfield, New Jersey 07621

Please send me the PLUME and MERIDIAN BOOKS I have checked above.
I am enclosing $_____(please add $1.50 to this order to cover
postage and handling). Send check or money order—no cash of C.O.D.'s.
Prices and numbers are subject to change without notice.

Name_____

Address_____

City_____State_____Zip Code_____
Allow 4-6 weeks for delivery.
This offer is subject to withdrawal without notice.